Robert Grant

The Opinions of a Philosopher

Robert Grant

The Opinions of a Philosopher

ISBN/EAN: 9783337072544

Printed in Europe, USA, Canada, Australia, Japan

Cover: Foto ©Thomas Meinert / pixelio.de

More available books at **www.hansebooks.com**

THE OPINIONS OF A PHILOSOPHER

BY
ROBERT GRANT

WITH AN ETCHING BY W. H. HYDE

NEW YORK
CHARLES SCRIBNER'S SONS
1895

THE OPINIONS OF A PHILOSOPHER

I

MY wife Josephine declares that I have become a philosopher in my old age, and perhaps she is right. Now that I am forty, and a trifle less elastic in my movements, with patches of gray about my ears which give me a more venerable appearance, I certainly have a tendency to look at the world as through a glass. Yet not altogether darkly be it said. That is, I trust I am no cynic like that fellow Diogenes who set the fashion centuries ago of turning up the nose at everything. I have a natural sunniness of disposition which would, I believe, be proof against the sardonic fumes of contemplation even though I were a real philosopher.

However, just as the mongoose of the bagman's story was not a real mongoose, neither am I a real philosopher.

You will remember that Diogenes, who was a real philosopher, occupied a tub as a permanent residence. He would roll in hot sand during the heat of summer, and embrace a statue of snow in winter, just to show his superiority to ordinary human conventions and how much wiser he was than the rest of the world. The real philosophers of the present day are not quite so peculiar; but they are apt to be fearfully and wonderfully superior to the weaknesses of humanity. For the most part they are to be found in the peaceful environs of a university or on some mountain top a Sabbath day's journey from the hum of civilization, where they eschew nearly everything which the every-day mortal finds requisite to comfort and convenience, unless it be whiskey and water. I have sometimes fancied that more real philosophers than we are aware of are partial on the sly to whiskey and water. But that is neither here nor there; for, as I have already stated, I am not a real philosopher.

I have altogether too many faults to be one, and should constantly be flying in the face of my own theories. Barring the aforesaid weakness for whiskey and water, it is fair to assume that the average real philosopher lives up to his own lights and by them; whereas I, at least according to Josephine, am liable to be frightfully inconsistent. She has never forgotten my profanity on the occasion when we discovered after dinner that the soot had come down in the drawing-room and was over everything in spite of the fact that the chimney had been swept three weeks before. Now, if there is one thing which I abhor and am perpetually inveighing against as vulgar and futile, it is unbridled language. Josephine must have heard me say fifty times if she has heard me one that the man who fouls his tongue with an oath is a senseless oaf. And yet I am bound to admit that when I discovered what had happened I swore deliberately and roundly like the veriest trooper.

In order to appreciate the situation exactly I should add that it has long been a mooted point between Josephine and me whether chimneys require to be swept at all. My darling insists that the sweep shall overhaul the house annually, while I cling, with what she is pleased to call masculine fatuity, to the theory that soot, like sleeping dogs, should be let alone.

Have you ever entered a drawing-room just after a healthy, thorough fall of soot? If so, you will appreciate what is meant by its all-pervasiveness. The remotest articles of furniture are rife with infinitesimal smut, much as they were rife with the remains of the lady in Kipling's story after the jealous orang-outang had done with her. And yet granting that the provocation was dire, a philosopher, a real philosopher, would have acted very differently. A philosopher of the grandest type would have reasoned that what was done was done, and that there was no more use in crying over fallen soot than over spilt milk. He would calmly have adopted prompt measures to ameliorate the situation, and after the servants were fairly at work would have taken his wife apart and pointed out to her, in well-chosen language, that here was only another instance of his superior wisdom. One of a more virulent type, but still a philosopher, might have indulged in mirth—quiet sarcastic mirth. No person of a truly philosophic cast of mind and with a rooted antipathy to damning would have sworn lustily as I did.

I remember taking little Fred, my namesake and eldest son, to skate with me one winter's afternoon on a suburban pond. He did famously for a tyro, but we both wearied at last of his everlasting strife to maintain the perpendicular, and I was conscious of a rush of joy when he became completely absorbed in watching a man who was fishing for pickerel. Have you ever fished for pickerel through a hole in the ice? If so you will recall that it is chilly and rather dispiriting work, especially if the fish are shy. They certainly were shy that afternoon, for the individual in question had angled long and bagged nothing, as I gleaned from the answers to the direct interrogatories put by my urchin during the few minutes I stood paternally by and watched the proceedings.

"Caught anything?"

"Nop."

"Had a bite?"

"Nop."

"How long you been fishing?"

"An hour."

As I glided away light-heartedly on the delicious curves of the outer edge, I reflected that he was evidently a persevering pot-hunter who would not be easily discouraged, and that I could count upon his engrossing the attention of my offspring for a considerable period. Accordingly, I was surprised some five minutes later to observe the fisherman (who wore no skates) shambling across the pond toward the shore. Glancing from him to his late station I perceived a little group of skaters gathered around my son and heir, who was dabbling with a stick in the abandoned hole. They appeared to be diverted by something, and one of them, my friend Harry Bolles, who had his handkerchief up to his mouth, made a bee-line to meet me. From his lips I learned what had happened, which was this wise : The horny-handed pot-hunter, having presently pulled a solitary pickerel out upon the ice and freed it from his hook, turned aside to cut another piece of bait ; whereupon my hopeful picked up the fish and popped it back into its native element without so much as a syllable of commentary ; and thereupon (being act three in the tragedy) he of the horny hand, having realized the situation in its terrible entirety, pulled up his line, shovelled back the particles of ice into the hole and betook himself upon his shambling way without one word. Not a word, mark you. There was a real philosopher, if you like, a thorough-going, square-trotting philosopher. The only alternative was child-murder or silence, and my pot-hunter chose the simplest form of the dilemma. "I thought the fish would like it," said little Fred, when interrogated upon the subject.

And yet, despite my occasional inability to practice what I preach, Josephine is correct in her diagnosis that my cast of mind is becoming more philosophic as the years roll on. The consciousness that I am the author of four children (two strapping sons and two tall daughters), anyone of whom may constitute me a grandfather before I am fifty, renders me conservative and disposed, metaphorically speaking, to draw in my horns a little. I am beginning to go to church again, for instance. You may have taken it for granted that I have been regular in my attendance at the sanctuary. Certainly I have never been a scoffer; but, on the other hand, I must confess that somehow it has come to pass since Josephine and I plighted our troth that our pew has stood empty on the Lord's day oftener than the orthodox consider fitting. And the worst of it is I used to attend service about every other Sabbath before I became a benedict, and Josephine taught a Sunday-school class up to within six months of our wedding ceremony. She, dear girl, has harbored ever since the belief that she continues to go to church almost every Sunday either in the morning or the afternoon, a harmless delusion which for some time I took no pains to dispel, knowing as I did that she meant to go every Sunday. Yet I knew also that pitiless, unemotional statistics would reveal an average attendance on her part of rather less than ten times in the course of each year. I was brute enough finally to call attention to a tally-sheet, covering a period of three calendar months, which I had kept for my private edification, and I was punished by seeing her sweet eyes fill with tears before she proceeded to plead to the indictment.

"You know, Fred, perfectly well that I have to stay at home with the children every other Sunday morning in order to allow Lucille to go to church."

"But how about the other mornings and all the afternoons?" I inquired, with the effrontery of a hardened sinner seizing his opportunity to take a saint to task.

Josephine blushed, partly from guilt and partly from indignation. "It rained torrents last Sunday morning, and Sunday morning fortnight—er—I was sick. I remember that I was all dressed to go one afternoon when old Mr. Philipps called and I didn't like to leave him. Besides, I feel as though I ought to stay at home occasionally on Sunday afternoons in order to teach the children the Scriptures. The Sunday morning before that—er—I went. No, it must have been a fortnight previous, for I recollect now that I had planned to go, when you said that you hated to skate alone and declined to take the entire responsibility of the children on the pond on account of little Fred and the pickerel."

"And I said, too, I remember, that in all probability there wouldn't be black ice again all winter."

"You did, you did," my darling cried, with tragic impetuosity, "and it is cruel of you to remind me of it."

"Moreover, it was a correct prophecy. It snowed that very night and the people who waited until Monday were nowhere."

"Oh, Fred, Fred, I'm a wicked woman. You're the last person in the world who ought to tax me with it, but it is true. I don't go to church as I ought. And yet I do mean to go. But if it isn't one thing which prevents, it's another. Lucille must have every other

Sunday morning, and you seem so disappointed if I refuse to go skating or canoeing with you and the children on the fine days that I foolishly yield."

"And you the daughter of a deacon," I continued, unsparingly. Let me state by way of explanation that Josephine's late father was for many years one of the pillars of the religious society to which he belonged.

"I know, I know. It is shameful. I—we are little better than heathens, Fred. Only think of it, four times in three months!" she added, glancing at the tell-tale sheet. "And I brought up to go regularly both morning and afternoon in addition to Sunday-school! I am a heathen; and as for you, I don't know what to call you!" she exclaimed, with a sad, reproachful smile.

So long as Josephine was content to berate herself without including me in her anathemas, I had been ready to acquiesce in what she said, but now that she seemed disposed to drag me into the conversation I felt it incumbent upon me to reply with dignity:

"Will you please explain, my dear, why it

is that, though I used to be a regular worshipper before we became man and wife, I have almost entirely ceased to attend church since that time? Who is responsible for the change, I wonder."

There is a point beyond which it is not safe to prod Josephine, and I could see from the expression of her eye that we had reached it on this occasion. She drew herself up and answered haughtily:

"I have heard you make that insinuation several times before, Fred. It is not merely silly, it is disgraceful. I keep you from church? Don't you know," she exclaimed, with a quaver of emotion, "that your refusal to go is a source of genuine grief to me, and that I just hate to go alone? Don't you know that I should like nothing better than to go with you every Sunday, and that I am ready to go to any church you will select?"

"Yes," I answered, doggedly, "I am well aware that you would prefer to have me become anything rather than remain—er—a steadfast worshipper of nature."

Josephine made a little gesture of impatience

such as my well-born apotheosis of nature is apt to evoke. For a few moments she looked as though she were going to cry ; then, with an almost passionate outburst, she exclaimed:

" You will promise me, Fred, won't you, that when the children are old enough to understand what it means not to go to church you will go too ? "

Now, it may be that my response at the time to this pathetic appeal was not altogether satisfactory to my darling ; but she has forgotten her fears and her tears to-day in the happy consciousness that as surely as the bells begin to ring on Sunday morning I begin to brush my silk hat with the feverish impatience of an abandoned church-goer. Punctuality, which has always seemed to Josephine a pitiful sort of virtue, ranks in my category of human conduct almost on a par with brotherly love, and I am apt to make myself and her pretty miserable on each returning Sabbath by my endeavors to get the family out of the house and into our pew on time. It is only by bearing strictly in mind what day it is that I am able to keep my lips from speaking guile when little Fred remembers at the last moment that he has forgotten his pocket-handkerchief or Josephine's glove bursts open in the process of being hastily rammed on and I am compelled to wait while she sends upstairs for a fresh pair. You should see how her nostrils swell with pride as we sweep by my old pal, Nicholas Long, and his wife, who are manifestly not going to church. I can discern on Nick's face, as we pass, an expression which is half sardonic, half pitiful. Evidently he has not forgotten my quondam oft-repeated vow that no child of mine should be taught the orthodox fairy tales in unlearning which I had spent some of the best years of my life. And now I am a recreant, and he who aided and abetted me in my asseverations of independence remains faithful. Yes, but Nick, poor fellow, has no children. His grin seems to say, "See what you are misssing, poor old patriarch ; Dorothy and I are off for a ten-mile tramp in the country."

Yet, despite his apparent jubilation of spirit, I detect a longing expression in Dorothy's eyes and I notice that she steals a second glance over her tailor-made shoulder at little Winona, our youngest, who is an uncommonly pretty child, if I do say it.

"There go a light-hearted, honest couple with the courage of their convictions," I remark to Josephine, tentatively. "Before the sermon has begun they will be on the river and they will come home delightfully tired just in time for dinner."

"Light-hearted? I believe, Fred, that they are both perfectly miserable," she exclaimed, with a sweeping glance of pride at her progeny. "I was thinking just before you spoke how much I pitied that woman."

I can remember as if it were yesterday Nick Long telling me with bubbling ecstasy, shortly after he was engaged, that his lady-love had a clear, analytical mind, almost like a man's. "No nonsense about her," he said. "She sees things just as they are." I rather got the impression at the time that he intended thereby to insinuate gently but plainly that he was a far luckier dog than I who had married a woman with a mind conspicuously feminine. I should like very much to know whether, if

Dorothy were to be blessed with children after all, Nick would have to go to church.

Not only have I lost moral courage in the matter of some of my deepest convictions, but I notice also with consternation that my physical bravery is ebbing away as my years increase. I have drawn the line, for example, squarely and tautly on burglars. One night not very long since I was awakened by noise and, after listening, I came to the conclusion that it proceeded from housebreakers. I slipped out of bed stealthily and put my ear to the bolted chamber door in order to confirm my conviction. My movements aroused Josephine, who sat up in bed and asked hoarsely what the matter was. I put my finger on my lips quite irrelevantly, for it was pitch dark.

"Fred, are there burglars in the house?" she gasped.

"Sh! Yes."

"What are you doing, Fred? Oh, you mus'n't go down and expose yourself on any account." She was evidently very much agitated. "Promise me that you will not."

Having ascertained that the door was secure I walked across the room and turned on the electric light. Josephine was sitting bolt upright, quivering with excitement. Her eyes followed my every movement, as, having slipped on my trousers and a pair of boots, I began to look around me, tramping sturdily.

"Fred, they'll hear you if you make such a noise," said my wife, in an agonized whisper.

"I fervently trust so," I retorted. "That's why I'm doing it."

As I spoke my eye lit at last on something adapted to my purpose. I had been trying to avoid the destruction of a wash basin, and I seized with grateful eagerness the pair of Indian clubs which offered themselves and, lifting them to the level of my brow, let them fall clamorously on the floor. The welkin rang, so to speak, and I sank with nervous exhaustion into an arm-chair.

The house seemed deathly still and it struck me that Josephine on her part was ominously quiet. When she spoke at last it was to ask:

"Haven't you a pistol?"

"Yes, dear."

"Are you going to let them take everything?"

"It is for them to decide, darling."

"But, Fred——" Josephine did not finish her sentence. The words she uttered were, however, so full of poignant surprise and disappointment that I felt constrained to inquire with a guilty attempt at nonchalance:

"Is there anything you would like to have me do?"

"You are the best judge, of course," she answered, coldly. "Only, do you think it is the usual way?"

"The usual way?" I echoed. Among the few points in Josephine's character which irritate me is her weakness for custom, and it is growing on her. "No, I suppose that the correct social thing would have been to stand at the head of the banisters in my nightgown with a lighted candle and make a target of myself."

"Why did you buy a pistol, then?" inquired my better half.

"So that the children needn't shoot themselves with it after it was locked up and the cartridges carefully hidden," I replied, with levity. We were both so heated that we had practically forgotten that flat burglary was supposed to be going on.

"You didn't use to talk in that way," said Josephine, with slow precision. "I only hope, Fred, for your sake that people won't hear about this."

"They will not, certainly, unless you tell them, Josephine."

"Tell them? I wouldn't mention what has happened for the world," she answered, looking at me with a sort of sorrowful disdain. Thus is it that the ideals which women form concerning us are one by one shattered! I am sure that Josephine would have been inconsolable had I fallen a victim to the bullet of a house-breaker. You will recall that her first impulse was to prevent me from exposing myself for the sake of the solid silver service. She had taken it for granted that I would slip the bolt and go part way down stairs, at least, pistol in hand, and she had wished to caution me against undue rashness. Consequently, it was a rude blow to her sensibilities to find that I was such a craven. She cared no more for our apostle spoons and gold-lined vegetable dishes than I did; it was the principle of the thing which distressed her. Why had I bought a six-shooter shortly after our marriage except to be equipped for just such an emergency? It did certainly seem that I was bound by all the laws of custom to pop at least once over the banisters, even though I took no aim and scurried back into my bedroom immediately after. That would have satisfied her, she subsequently admitted to me; but to drop a pair of Indian clubs on the floor in order to make a clatter could be regarded as little less than pusillanimous, philosophy or no philosophy.

We have talked it over many times since, and I have endeavored to make plain to her that in the process of evolution thinking men have come to the conclusion that the husband and father who chops logic at dead of night with an accomplished burglar on the wrong side of his chamber door is akin to a lunatic. She listens to my arguments attentively, and she has done me the honor to admit that there is more to be said in my behalf than she thought at first ; but I remember that the last time we conversed upon the subject she shook her head with the air of a woman who, in spite of everything, is still of the same opinion, and she murmured gently :

"As I told you before, Fred, if you had fired once over the banisters, I would say nothing."

"But I might have been killed or maimed for life as a consequence," I blurted, feelingly.

Josephine looked a little grave, as she is apt to do at any suggestion of my sudden taking off, but with a sweet sigh she answered, succinctly :

" There are certain risks in this world that a man has to take."

II

YOU may remember that I have four children; my namesake Fred, David, who was christened in honor of his maternal grandfather, Josephine, or Josie as we call her in order not to confound her with her mother, and Winona, the baby of the family. We have lately moved into another house. The old one would not hold us any longer. At least Josephine declared that it would not shortly after the agents of the Board of Health fumigated the establishment with sulphur to kill scarlet-fever germs. She said it would be cheaper to move than to buy new wall-papers and window-shades. When I asked how this could be she waxed a little wroth at what she called my density, and asked if I did not appreciate that we should have to move at any rate in a year or two in order to provide the children with a bedroom apiece. The necessity for this had not occurred to me, I must confess, and I was making bold to inquire why the two boys could not continue to occupy one room and their sisters another as in the past, when Josephine added, in an awful whisper:

"Besides, the house is overrun with cockroaches. Now mind, Fred," she continued, with an imperative frown, "that is a matter which is not to be repeated to anyone."

"Why should I wish to repeat it?" I asked, meekly.

"I never know beforehand what you will repeat and what you will not. I should expect to hear from Jemima Bolles the next time we met that you had confided it to her husband, and positively I don't care to have her know. Then, too," Josephine continued, with the manner of one selecting a few of many grievances to air, "I haven't an inch of unoccupied closet room; and, moreover, you remember, Fred, that the plumber said the last time he was here that by good rights the plumbing ought all to be renewed." My wife dwelt on these concluding words with insinuating emphasis. She knows that I am daft, as she calls it, on two points, closing windows on the eve of a thunder-shower and defective drainage.

"He said that we could manage very well for some time longer without the slightest real risk," I answered, doughtily.

Josephine's lower lip trembled. Presently she burst out, as though she had resolved to throw feline argument and sophistic persuasion to the winds, "I am just tired of this house, Fred, and I should like to move tomorrow. It is pitifully small and disgustingly dirty with dirt that I can't get rid of, and everything about it is old as the hills. It has never been the same place since that fall of soot. If I am obliged to live in it I shall have to, but I am sure that a new, clean house would add ten years to my life."

"Jehosophat!" I added, startled by this appeal into borrowing the latest expletive from the vocabulary of my eldest son, at which Josephine bridled for an instant, thinking that she had detected blasphemy. When it dawned upon her that the phrase in question was only one of those hybrid, meaningless objurgations, the use of which will scarcely justify a lecture, my darling gulped dismally and waited for me to go on.

I am inclined to think that a gradually evolved tendency of mine not to go on when I am expected to was what first prompted my wife to dub me a philosopher. She fancies, dear soul, that she is a loser by this lately developed proclivity to seek refuge in silence on the occasions when she or the children sweep down upon me with some hair-lifting project which craves an immediate decision. But she is in error. It is true there are times when the sweet onslaught of the sons and daughters of my house and their mother has brought the old man to terms on the spot, and wrung from him an immediate permission to do or to spend; but, on the other hand, Josephine, who in spite of her cunning is no philosopher, and her offspring little realize how often their feelings have been saved from laceration by this trick of mine (she calls it a trick) of saying nothing until I have had time for reflection. No man is so wise as his wife and children combined, but it takes him a little while to find it out; and I have discovered that to chew a matter over and over is the surest way to avoid promulgating a stern refusal.

So it was in this instance. Had I uttered the words which rose to my lips, I should have felt obliged to inform Josephine that, her premature taking off to the contrary notwithstanding, to move into another house was out of the question and totally unnecessary. How could I afford to move? Why should we move? The dear old house where we had passed so many joyous years and which Josephine used to say was extraordinarily convenient! I remember that I became successively irate, pathetic, and bumptious in my secret soul. I said to myself stoutly that it was all nonsense, and that by means of a little fresh paint and new coverings for the dining-room chairs, we should be happy where we were for another five years.

Cockroaches? Bah! Was there not insect powder?

The married man who knows in his secret soul that he cannot afford to move and who has made up his mind that nothing on earth shall induce him to, is terribly morose for the first few weeks after his wife has unbosomed herself upon the subject. He peruses with a savage frown the real estate columns of the daily newspapers, while he mutters vicious sentences such as, "I'll be blessed if I will!" or, "Not if I know myself, and I think I do!" He observes moodily every house in process of erection, and scrutinizes those "To Let" with an animosity not quite consistent with his determination to put his foot down for once and crush the whole project in the bud. Why is it that he slyly visits after business hours the outlying section of the city, where the newest and most desirable residences are offered at fashionable prices? Why at odd moments does he make rows of figures on available scraps of paper and on the blotter at his office, and abstractedly compute interest on various sums at four and a half and five per cent.? Why? Because the leaven of his wife's threat that her life will be shortened is working in his bosom and he beholds her in his restless dreams crushed to death beneath a myriad of waterbugs, all for the lack of an inch of closet-room. Why? Because he is haunted perpetually by the countenances of his daughters, on which he reads sorrowfully written that they are wasting away for lack of the bedchamber apiece promised them by their mother. Why? Because, in brief, he is a philosopher, and recognizes that what is to be is to be, and that it is easier to dam up the waters of the Nile with bulrushes (to adopt an elegant and well-seasoned exemplar of impossibility) than to check the progress of maternal pride.

Some four months after Josephine's announcement that she would live ten years longer elsewhere, I returned home one afternoon with what she subsequently stigmatized as a sly expression about the corners of my mouth. I doubt if I did look sly, for I pride myself on my ability to control my features when it is necessary. However that may be, having persuaded Josephine to take a walk, I conducted her to the door of a newly finished house in the fashionable quarter.

"It might be amusing to go in and look it over," I murmured. "I should rather like to see the ramifications of a modern house."

Josephine, albeit a little surprised, was enraptured. She promptly took the lead and I tramped at her side religiously from cellar to attic, while she peeped into all the closets and investigated the laundry and kitchen accommodations and drew my attention to the fact that the furnace and the ice-chest would be amply separated.

"You know, Fred, that in our house they are side by side and we use a scandalous amount of ice as a consequence," she said, hooking her arm in mine lovingly.

"The whole house strikes me as very well arranged," I retorted, in a bluff tone, as much as to say that I saw through her blandishments. I think she appreciated this. Nevertheless, a few minutes later when we were on the dining-room story, she rubbed her head against my shoulder and said, "Just see what a love of a pantry, Fred. Mine is a hole compared to it. Servants in a house like this would never leave one. And do look at this ceiling. It is simple, but divinely clean and appropriate."

"It is well enough," said I, coldly.

After indulging in various other raptures, to which I seemed to turn a deaf ear, and examining everything to her heart's discontent, Josephine moved toward the front door with a sigh. Then it was that I remarked:

"So the house suits you, my dear?"

"It is ideal," she murmured, "simply ideal."

"There are things about it which I don't fancy altogether," said I.

"Oh, Fred, if we only had a house like it, I should be perfectly satisfied."

"Should you? It is yours," I answered.

"Don't be unkind, Fred."

"It is yours," I repeated, a little more explicitly.

Josephine devoured me with inquiring eyes. As she gazed, the expression of my countenance brought the blood to her cheeks and she cried with the plaintiveness of a wounded animal, "What do you mean, dear? It is cruel of you to make sport of me."

"I am not making sport of you, Josephine. The house is yours—ours. I bought it yesterday. Here is the deed, if you mistrust me," I continued, solemnly drawing from my pocket the document in question.

Josephine took it like one dazed. She looked from me to it and back again from it to me, then with a joyous laugh she exclaimed, "Really? It is really true? Oh, Fred, you are an angel!"

"No, my dear," I answered, as she flung her arms about my neck—for she does so still once in a while—"I am merely a philosopher who has learned to recognize that what must be must be."

My wife was too much absorbed in her own mysterious mental processes to take note of or analyze this observation. For a few moments she was lost in a brown study, and gazed about her with a glance that struck me as somewhat critical.

"You are an angel, Fred," she repeated,

ruminantly. "You took me in splendidly, didn't you? And to think of your doing it all by yourself!"

She wandered back into the dining-room, and thence to the hall, where she stood peering up the stairway at the skylight. "Yes," she continued presently, in a judicial, contemplative tone, "I think it will do very well on the whole. I am not perfectly sure that the laundress will be satisfied with the arrangement of the laundry, and I don't see exactly, Fred, what you are to do for a dressing-room, when we have more than one visitor. I am out of conceit with the tinting of the drawing-room ceiling, and—and several of the mantelpieces are hideous. But, on the other hand, the dining-room is perfectly lovely, there is no end of closet-room, and the kitchen is a gem. Oh, thank you, Fred, thank you ever so much. I really never expected that we could afford to leave the dear old house. It will almost break my heart to leave it, too, although it is so dirty."

Josephine's guns were spiked, as it were. Having declared that the house was ideal, she was barred from utterly blasting it in the next breath. To tell the truth, I felt as a consequence decidedly perky and inclined to perform the double-shuffle or something of the sort quite out of keeping with the traditional repose of a philosopher. It was so obvious to me that I had escaped weeks, if not months, of misery by the ruse which I had adopted that I was fain to dance with joy. Had I allowed Josephine to pick out a house she would have felt obliged, even though she was thoroughly satisfied with the first she saw, to inspect from top to bottom every other in the market, for fear that she might see something which pleased her better, and I should have been compelled to accompany her. There are a few advantages after all in being of a philosophic turn of mind.

And here is another bit of philosophy for you which I am thoroughly convinced is sound. A woman adroitly handled will permit her husband to choose a new unfurnished house for her without serious demur. But let the lord and master beware who takes it upon himself to do the furnishing also stealthily and of his own accord. I will confess that it did occur to me at first to put through the whole business at one fell swoop—house, wall-papers, dados, chandeliers, carpets, and curtains. I even went so far as to cross the street one day with the intention of asking Poultney Briggs, who makes a business of letting people know what they ought to like in the line of interior decoration, to name his price to complete the job. But my courage failed me at the last minute, for I had a presentiment that Josephine would be disappointed if I did. You see I know her pretty well after all these years.

"I should never have forgiven you, Fred— never!" said my better-half, emphatically, when I told her how near I had come to the crucial act. "I should have hated everything. Besides, no one nowadays thinks anything of Poultney Briggs as a decorator. He is terribly behind the times."

I accepted this reproof and the accompanying verdict with becoming meekness. I remember that when we first went to housekeeping Poultney Briggs was in the van of artistic progress, and that no one was to be mentioned in the same breath with him; yet now, apparently, he was of the sere-and-yellow-leaf order, professionally speaking. And I was old fogy enough not to have been aware of it. Clearly, I was not fit to be entrusted with the selection of even a door-mat, to say nothing of the wall-papers and carpets. It was with a thankful heart over my foresight that I relinquished to Josephine the whole task of furnishing, with the sole reservation that I should have my say about the wine-cellar. My only revenge, a miserable one forsooth, was that she resembled a skeleton three months later; a pale, pitiful bag of bones, though proud and radiant withal. Had it not been for that prediction that her life was to be lengthened, I should have felt anxious. What a marvellous creation a woman is, to be sure! Man and philosopher as I am, my impulse would have been to consign the contents of the garret to the auctioneer or the ash-man, and to retain most of the least-used furniture and upholstery to eke out our new splendor. But Josephine's method was distinctly opposite. She was critical of nearly everything respectable-looking in the old house ; on the other hand, there was scarcely anything in the attic or lumber-room, where our useless things were stored, which did not turn out to be a treasure and just the thing for the new establishment. To begin with, there was a love of a set of andirons and a brass fender (to reproduce Josephine's description exactly), which had been discarded at the time we began housekeeping as too old-fashioned and peculiar. Of equal import was a disreputable-looking mahogany desk with brass handles and claw feet which had belonged to my great-grandmother before it was banished to the garret within a month after our wedding ceremony, on the plea that none of the drawers would work. They don't still, for that matter. A cumbersome, stately Dutch clock and a toast-rack of what Josephine styled mediæval pattern, were among the other discoveries. The latter was reposing in a soap-box in company with a battered, vulgar nutmeg-grater. But the pieces of resistance, as I called them, on account of the difficulty we had in moving them from behind a pile of old window-blinds, were the portraits of a little gentleman in small-clothes, with his hair in a cue and a seeming cast in one eye, and a stout lady with a high complexion and corkscrew ringlets.

"Oh, Fred, who are they?" cried Josephine, ecstatically, and she began to dust the seedy, frameless canvases with a reverential air. "Where did they come from?"

"They're ancestors of mine, love."

"Ancestors? How lovely, Fred! I didn't know you had any. I mean I didn't know you had any who had their portraits painted."

"On the contrary, Josephine, I told you who they were when we were engaged, and I remember I was rather anxious to hang them in the dining-room, but you said they were a pair of old frumps, and that you wouldn't give them house space. So we compromised on the attic."

"Did I?" said my darling, gravely. "Well it must have been because the dining-room was too small for them. They will look delightfully in our new one, when they are mounted and touched up a bit, and they will set off our Copley of my great-aunt in the turban. What are their names? They must have names."

"They are my great-grandfather Plunkett and his wife, on my father's side. He was a common hangman."

"Now don't be idiotic, Fred."

"He was, my dear. It was you yourself who said it. Don't you remember my calling two of your forbears a precious pair of donkeys because they wouldn't eat any form of shell-fish, and your replying that, though I was in the habit of grandiloquently describing my ancestor who used to execute people as 'the sheriff of the county,' he was only a common hangman?"

"Oh, was that the man? All I said was that if he had been *my* ancestor instead of yours, you would have called him a hangman. He *was* sheriff of the county, wasn't he, dear?"

"So I have been taught to believe."

"'My ancestor, the high sheriff,' won't sound badly at all," she said, jauntily.

"Especially if we can tone up the old gentleman's game eye a little."

Josephine's face expressed open admiration. "You are a genius and a duck," she exclaimed; then, after a reflective pause, she murmured, "Very likely he met with an accident just before he was painted."

"Yes, dear. Consequently, if the eye can't be improved by means of the best modern artistic talent, the least we can do is to put a shade over it."

This waggish remark seemed to be lost on Josephine. She wore a far-away look as though her thoughts were following some fancy which had appealed to her. She did not deign to take me into her confidence at the moment, but a fortnight later I happened to come upon her in close confabulation with a very clever, rising, local artist, over this same portrait of my great-grandfather Plunkett.

"Fred," she said, nonchalantly, "Mr. Binkey thinks he can do something to this which will improve it."

"I shouldn't suppose that it was easy to improve upon nature," I remarked, oracularly.

Josephine blushed a little, but she replied, with sturdy decision, "Oh, but he never could have looked like that. His eyes must have been alike, Fred. Mustn't they, Mr. Binkey?"

"I should imagine," said our rising local artist, with a meditative squint at the picture, "that the fault was in the technique rather than in the subject-matter of the portrait."

"Precisely," said Josephine, triumphantly. "Besides, Mr. Binkey says it needs varnishing."

What can one say in the teeth of professional authority? When great-grandfather and great-grandmother Plunkett came back to us at the end of a month, they were newly varnished and in bright, tasteful frames, and no one would ever have detected that the old gentleman's eyes did not resemble each other closely. Since then I have often heard Josephine declare her gratitude that she did not allow any squeamishness to prevent her from giving the children and people generally the correct impression of a man who was eminent in his day and generation. Indeed,

I have heard her call the attention of visitors to the strong similarity about the brow and eyes which our second son David bears to his great-grandfather, High Sheriff Plunkett, and I do not question in the least that she believes the cast in the old gentleman's optic never to have existed save in the original portrait-painter's imagination. I must admit that, notwithstanding the changes made by local talent in my ancestor's physiognomy, I am occasionally struck myself with the strong resemblance specified by Josephine; and the longer I live the less doubt I have that she is a far cleverer person than your humble servant.

III

SHORTLY before we moved to the seaside this summer, it was evident to me that Josephine had something on her mind which she hesitated to broach to me. I suspect that the dear girl realized that we had had rather a trying winter in our new establishment, and was accordingly a little nervous as to how I would receive a new suggestion, which was aimed directly at my personal comfort. I had indeed found the winter somewhat trying on account of the number of small repairs which had proved to be necessary. Most of the doors would not open except by the application of brute force, and many of the windows rattled, so that carpenters were in possession of the premises a total of one hundred and twenty-eight hours in the course of nine calendar months, and I was compelled to listen in hang-dog silence to Josephine's sibilant commentary, that this was the natural result of buying a ready-made house. Still, I must admit that on the whole she behaved extraordinarily well under these trying circumstances, and said nothing more tart than that, if she ever were so foolish as to move again, she should insist on building a house to suit herself; which struck me as rather a boomerang of a speech, seeing that it implied a lurking doubt on her part as to whether she had been wise in moving at all. I even came near admitting to her in consequence that I was thankful we had moved, and that, surface indications to the contrary notwithstanding, I was extremely happy in my new surroundings, and egregiously proud of her taste and cleverness in the selection of wall-papers and upholstery. I could have truthfully added also that, though a slippery hump had replaced the cosey hollow in my renovated easy-chair, I had found one of the new chairs exactly suited to my sensibilities, and should be secretly pleased if the old one were to softly and suddenly vanish away during our absence at the sea-side, after the manner of the Boojum of ditty. I have really no adequate reason to give why I delayed to make this amiable confession. It was the consciousness, however, that I had it to make which had prompted me to help my darling out of her quandary when I perceived that she seemed afraid to beard the lion in his den.

"It has been very evident to me, Josephine, for the last two days, that you are keeping back something. If your mind is really set on altering the tinting of the drawing-room ceiling, I will consent to have it done while we are out of town."

"It isn't that at all, Fred. I agree with you that we can't afford it this year."

"Is it the extra tub in the laundry, then?"

"Of course it would be very nice if we could have an extra tub. But it isn't that."

"Then there is something?"

"Yes," she murmured. "Oh, Fred, I do hope, now that the doctor has ordered you to take more exercise, you will get one of those pretty, striped, tennis suits."

"Yes, do, father dear," exclaimed my eldest daughter, who happened to enter the room at the moment and overheard her mother's speech. "You would look perfectly lovely in one."

"It would be a satisfaction for once to see you wear something a little joyous," continued my wife, emboldened by the enthusiasm of her offspring.

"You seem to forget, dear, that I am a plain man," I answered, though to tell the truth I was asking myself whether I was not a trifle weary of posing in that sublime capacity. Now that I thought of it, what was the especial virtue of being a plain citizen?

When I came to reflect on the matter further, I realized that my programme for the past fifteen years has been to put on a plain pepper-and-salt suit of modest demeanor in the morning, eat two plain-boiled eggs for breakfast, walk down town in a plain black overcoat to my office in a plain-looking building, where I pursue my calling until it is time to go home and doff my pepper-and-salt of modest demeanor for a plain suit of sables, the funereal dress-clothes of commerce and convention. Even this coal-black tribute to ceremony has discredited me with some, who argue that I am not a plain man because I do not prefer to dine in the same old pepper-and-salt. Verily the only bits of warm color in my wardrobe have been a robin's-egg-blue neck-tie, which I have never dared to wear except once at a wedding, and a pair of pajamas reserved for very occasional jaunts on yachts and sleeping cars. And now that I had the doctor's orders to take more exercise, I had been on the point of selecting an ordinary, plain, pepper-and-salt flannel shirt, and condemning one of my oldest and plainest pairs of pepper-and-salt trousers for the purpose.

And yet it was not always so. I remember that when I was a young fellow and a bachelor I used to be, if not a dandy exactly, very particular regarding my personal appearance, and that I was willing to approach the border line of gaudiness as closely as any of my contemporaries. It took courage, too, then : the youth who wore down town even a garden flower in his button-hole was liable to be suspected of a lack of purpose. One got very little encouragement at the best in any effort to fly in the face of the perpetual black tie and black broadcloth frock-coat of the plain American citizen, and he who chose not to wear the garb of the Republic not merely cut himself off from the possibility of ever becoming President, but ran the risk of being refused employment of any kind. Naturally, therefore, I began after I was married to do pretty much as the rest of my fellow-citizens did, save in the matter of a dress-coat at dinner, which I continued to don daily out of respect to Josephine's feelings. (This has been one of the few points in my behavior upon which she has ever laid particular stress, and I thank her here publicly for her pertinacity. It has saved me from the slough of utter carelessness.) Barring the single blue necktie and the pajamas, I drifted into and have stuck to blacks and browns and the least ostentatious cuts until my own wife and children have felt called upon to proclaim me fusty.

To tell the truth, I had been more or less

conscious for some time of my degeneration in this respect, but it is no easy matter to escape from a rut when one is middle-aged. Josephine's stricture concerning the lack of joyousness in my apparel, however, brought me up standing, as the phrase is, and served not merely to spur me to action, but to chrystallize a tissue of reflections which had been churning in my brain during a considerable period. One evening a fortnight later I sauntered into the drawing-room, where my wife and four children were congregated round the family lamps, and drew attention to my appearance by a timorous cough.

Josephine was the first to look up. My foot-fall will usually draw from her a welcoming smile, but she happened to be absorbed at the moment in the end of a novel, the beginning of which she was going to read later, so that it was not until I coughed that she raised her eyes from her book. For a moment she stared at me as though she were doubtful whether I was not one of the characters in whose vicissitudes she had been engrossed, then, letting the volume fall to the ground, she exclaimed in a voice of rapture, "Children, look at your father!"

Roused from their respective volumes by the ardor of this exhortation, my two sons and two daughters bent their critical eyes upon the male author of their being. It was a moment of sweet triumph for the old man for which he had made the most careful preparations. It was in vain that their gimlet-like faculties sought to discover flaws in the eminently fashionable costume of white striped serge, the brand-new yellow shoes, the jaunty summer necktie, and the appropriate hat, whereby I was transformed from a plain man to a respectable-looking member of society. The father who can run the gauntlet of his children's censorship may look the cold world in the face without a quaver. Philosophy has taught me this, and it was under the spur of the philosophic spirit that I had sought out the most expensive and most fashionable tailor in town, and told him to build me a summer outfit such as no one could carp at. Expense? He was to spare none. Cut? The latest and most joyous.

The children clapped their hands and there

was a lively chorus of approval, and I had the satisfaction of hearing Josie, whose hair is ornamently auburn, and whose face reminds me of her mother at the same age, declare that I looked "perfectly scrumptious," a sentiment which, in spite of its flavor of school-girl slang, seemed to express the critical estimate of the family circle.

"I look like a perfect idiot," I remarked, with becoming modesty, as I surveyed myself in the glass. I did not think so, all the same. Indeed, I was saying to myself that I had had no idea I could look so well. Yet, after all, it is other people who decide whether one looks like an idiot or not.

"On the contrary," said Josephine, having surveyed me once more from head to foot to make sure that I was in nowise peculiar, but just like everybody else (only nicer, as she would say), " you look neat, and cool as a cucumber, and five years younger. Doesn't he, dears?"

"I should think so," said little Fred, who is aiming to be a dandy himself. "Father has cut us all out completely."

"It is a comfort to think that I shall no longer be a disgrace to my family," I remarked with humble mien. "I may add that this is not all. I possess not merely this costume, but I have replenished my wardrobe utterly. When you see my new trousers, my new summer overcoat, my assortment of neckties, my brilliant shoes—both patent leather and strawberry roan—you will no longer be able to state, Josephine, that my clothes lack joyousness."

Later in the evening, after the children had gone to bed, Josephine, who had been up stairs to inspect my purchases, sat down beside me on the sofa, and nestled her head against my shoulder.

"Fred, you are very good," she said. "It must have bothered you terribly to get all those things—you, who are so busy. Everything is lovely, and the latest and prettiest of its kind. You have shown exquisite taste, dear; but I feel as though I had badgered you into it, following as it does on top of the house and everything else."

"No, dearest," I answered, stroking her

hair. "I am proud of you—I am grateful to you. A man falls behind the times before he is aware of it. The world changes and paterfamilias ought to change with it out of consideration for his children. You were perfectly right, Josephine, just as you were right about the moving. Our house was too small and I was getting to look fusty and frowsy."

"Not so bad as that, Fred. I never said that you didn't look perfectly clean and respectable. All I meant was that there are such pretty things now, it seems a pity not to wear them. It wasn't the fashion to wear them when you were young. I mean younger than you are now," she added, patting my cheek. "I am glad, Fred, that you are reconciled to the house. I know that I have been a thorn in your flesh for the last eighteen months on account of it. I didn't mean to be irritating about the moving, but I was, and my soul has been wearing sackcloth and ashes ever since because I was so nasty. You see, Fred, in the first place, though I pretended to be pleased at your selecting the house, I was really dreadfully disappointed, for half the fun of a new house is choosing it. Of course a new house chosen by some one else is better than none at all, but a woman hates surprises of that sort, and somehow my teeth were set on edge by the few things about the house that didn't suit me. And then, dear," she continued, caressingly, "I don't think it was very nice of me to meddle with your great-grandfather Plunkett's portrait. It was too much in the line of the people who have their ancestors painted to order. I think of it quite often at night and blush, which shows that I have a guilty conscience on the subject, though I can't help feeling that it has been very much improved whenever I look at it."

"It was a very trifling amelioration," I answered. "And, if I remember rightly, it was I who put you up to it."

"Yes, but you were only in jest, and I was base enough to adopt the idea and act upon it. No, Fred, though I agree that everything has worked out a great deal more satisfactorily than I deserve, and that we are infinitely better off than we have ever been before in point of comfort and general happiness, I look back on the last year and a half as a sort of nightmare. You were content to live along steadily in the dear old house and to toil unselfishly for us all, and I was perpetually prodding you. It has made me feel myself to be a perfect ogre of a woman. And yet it seemed to me to be necessary, Fred."

"It was not merely necessary, Josephine. It was essential. Thank goodness we have got through it so lightly! It is not every man who survives the operation. But, as I have said to you already, I am the one who should be grateful, and I too was the one at fault. Had you waited for me to make the suggestion, we should have been still in that dirty little box of a house, and I should have been wearing the same black wisp of a necktie such as I have worn for the last fifteen years. Kiss me, darling."

She did so, and as she leaned her head lovingly against my breast she looked up and said, tremulously: "It was all on account of the children, Fred. I wish them to have every chance there is." There spoke the fond mother-bird. The children ! Are these young giants and giantesses our children ? Seemingly but yesterday they were little tots pottering in the sand with spade and shovel, alternately angelic and demoniac, supplying annual testimony to the inability of green apples to oppress a hardy digestion, and free from every inkling of responsibility save a faint, intermittent respect for parental mandate. Now they tower before me in the glory of budding manhood and maidenhood ; lovable, yet haughty ; with star-like eyes and brows perplexed by all the problems of the universe ; God-like in their devotion to principle, though distressingly eager for pocket-money.

"Fred," whispers the dear woman at my side, breaking in upon my cogitation, "what were you like as a boy—er—a young man, I mean ? "

Her words are the answering echo to my own secret thought. Like myself she is groping for light and counsel. May not the cleverest man and woman fitly quail before the soul-hunger of eager adolescent youth? And I do not profess to be clever.

"What were you like as a young woman?"

"I was afraid you would make that answer," she murmurs, reproachfully. "Oh, I have forgotten!"

"And if we could remember, Josephine, it would not help us very much. Each generation finds the world a virgin field. Somehow, though, I had fancied that when we had seen them through the scarlet fever and landed them in college, it would be plain sailing. We have to begin all over again, though, and the second half promises to be the most difficult."

"I know it. And think how we worried, or rather tried not to worry, over them when they were little things, and how we fancied there were no problems to compare in difficulty with supplying them with proper food and proper masters. In the last fifteen years they have had everything — chicken-pox, measles, whooping-cough, mumps, and scarlet fever. And they've collected everything —postage-stamps, minerals, butterflies, coins, and cigarette pictures. And they've kept everything—rabbits, goats, bull-terriers, white mice, a pony, and guinea-pigs."

"And owned, and subsequently discarded, to my certain knowledge, a music-box, doll's-house, puppet-show, printing-press, steam-engine, aquarium, and camera."

"Yes, and over and above their school learning they've been taught to swim, ride, dance, use tools, play on the piano, and speak fair to middling French. Yet, as you say, Fred, the most difficult part is to come, just as we fancied that we were through. And the terrible reflection is that we're not so sure now what we ought to do for them as we were when they were younger."

"Precisely, dear."

"And it seems sometimes very strange to me, Fred, that though they've eaten out of the same dish, as it were, all their days, and had the same opportunities, they should be so totally unlike one another physically, mentally, and morally. It's impossible to lay down any hard-and-fast rule for them now, as one could do when they were little."

It is indeed. I see them on the threshold of manhood and maidenhood looking up to my wife and me for guidance and counsel, though they pretend to be sufficient to themselves in matters of judgment. A word of encouragement or of disapproval from us may be the turning-point in their destinies, may set the seal on what they are to become. Even as the flowers are drawn by the sun and the willows follow the prevailing wind, their young lives may be turned to good or saved from ill by our loving sympathy or remonstrance in the nick of time. We clinch our fingers in the stress of uncertainty. Good counsel? Yes, a thousand times yes; but who will counsel the counsellors?

How the world has changed since Josephine and I were their age! More particularly that choicest section of it which we were taught to think and speak of as the land of the free and the home of the brave. As I look back now in philosophic mood, simplicity seems to me to have been the keynote of our day. Not merely had the gladsome flannel costume and the Indian pajamas not yet begun to force an issue with the oratorical black broadcloth coat and the up-and-down white nightgown. There were no shingle stains to speak of but those of time and eternity, and he who owned a vehicle of any kind must needs be careful that it was of sombre hue and homely pattern. Among the fixed truths which we imbibed with the maternal milk, and from the prejudice of which I never expect to be wholly free, were these: That though the blatant blast of the Western politician offend the sensitive ear of culture by exaggeration, it is still true that we are the greatest nation under the sun by virtue of our total disregard of everything which other nations have held fast to; that the American woman is a newly created species; that George Washington never told a lie; that though France was on our side in our struggle for Independence, for which we should ever be profoundly grateful, the custom of handing over young people to be married at parental dictate, coupled with certain hoarse suspicions of an unmentionable character, must be an everlasting barrier between us and the Gaul; that, nevertheless, if a man will have his fling, he may do so in Paris once without being held to strict account for it, provided that he comes home and lives a respectable life ever after on this side the water; that Russia's ill-treatment of the serf and general barbaric conditions are to be overlooked on account of the friendliness she displayed toward us in our hour of need, barbarism being on the whole a less crucial blemish than the above-mentioned peculiarities of our other ally; and that everyone should hitch his wagon to a star.

In this last injunction lay, perhaps, the gist of the whole matter. To hitch one's wagon to a star was to be, primarily, a plain person, to go in for truth, patriotism, fineness of soul, long hours of labor, little exercise and no vacations, pies and doughnuts, ugliness of physical surroundings, and squeaky feminine voices. Public opinion justified making all the money one could, provided it was not spent in rendering life ornate or beautiful. So lived our fathers and mothers, our upright, vigorous, single-minded, ascetic predecessors ; and in our day their precepts were still held in reverence. Yet even then there were indications of a change. The newly created species took it into her head to look around her, especially in summer, first by itineraries along the rock-bound coast of her native land, and later by amazon-like pilgrimages abroad. She invented Bar Harbor, and while electrified Europe held its breath perambulated Paris alone and climbed Mont Blanc with a single man. She also made the pertinent discovery that her popper's purse was pudgy with the proceeds of wheat, corn, dry goods, and railway shares. Though she still urged the successive youths who strolled and sat under her Japanese sunshade to hitch their wagons to heavenly bodies, she gave it sweetly, and little by little to be understood that chastity among women and high resolve among men need not preclude more picturesque paraphernalia and a broader field of investigation. She bought French clothes ; her brothers took the hint from her, and hied them to Paris and Vienna to pursue their studies ; penetrated to Pekin and Constantinople, and hunted the tiger in the jungles of India, while popper's pudgy purse grew more and more plethoric despite the drafts upon it. Purification by pie waned, and the first Queen Anne cottage reared its head.

I wooed and won Josephine in those early, transitory days when the influence of the past was still upon us, though we foresaw and caught glimpses of the new. We were simple souls. I believe that Josephine's wagon was hitched to a star ; else I could not have loved her. And she believed the same of mine. She wandered in the panoply of her maiden independence to far-off rookeries attended by me only (or some other swain only). Though we were fain to discuss De Musset and Herbert Spencer, Darwin and Dobson, George Eliot and Philip Gilbert Hamerton—strange names to the elder generation—our scheme of life was still essentially grave and plain for all Josephine's Japanese sunshade and tendency to make the most of her willowy figure. Little did we dream of the later development which, like a huge wave, was to sweep over the land of the free and the home of the brave, overwhelming its native simplicity with the virtues, tastes, and vices of the other nations against which our forefathers barred the door. Palaces in all but the name stand where the buffalo was wont to disport himself, and where the American eagle in human form once flapped his wings and screamed most viciously in contempt of the effete civilization of the older world. Sons and daughters of the pioneers who bolted their dinners on the stroke of twelve find seven too early for elegant convenience. Among the reddest and palest of hot-house roses, which deck their tables, glisten glass of Venetian pattern and china from the bankrupt stock of kings. According to their intellectualities their talk is of labor and capital, of working-girls' clubs and model tenement-houses, of Buddha and Zola, of foreign titles, and transplanted fox-hunting. To-day a hundred thousand dollars is barely a competency, and a building less than a dozen stories high dwarfs the highway of trade. The vestibule limited, the ocean greyhound, the Atlantic cable, and the voice-bearing telephone have made all nations kin, and bid fair to amalgamate society. Even the newly created species condescends to swap her birthright for a coronet.

All this has come to pass while Josephine and I have been plodding along the route of all flesh, trying not to forget our early aspirations. We have changed our dinner-hour with the rest of the world; we have learned to talk more or less unintelligently about the sweating system and Buddhism; we have bowed our necks to the yoke of the electric wire. Now that Josephine has spurred me on to it, I have even bought a modern house, and replenished my wardrobe so as to keep pace with thought and custom. But, nevertheless, sitting here in my renovated easy-chair, with my feet stretched toward the brass andirons which were the pride of one of my great-grandmothers, listening to the ticking of the old-fashioned clock which belonged to another of them, and conscious that the eyes of my most distinguished ancestor are looking down at me from the wall, I feel bewildered, as it were, by this latter-day metamorphosis, bristling with new and formidable problems. Whither is civilization tending? What is one to think of it all? And by the shades of my forefathers, purified by pie, how shall we best help our sons and daughters to hitch their wagons to stars? That is what is worrying Josephine and me.

IV

WE have just faced our first serious problem.

Said my wife to me one day not long ago, handing me the newspaper as she spoke, "Look at this, my dear. Little Fred has been selected to play on the University foot-ball eleven."

By way of contradistinction to me, who am rather short and slight, my namesake and eldest son is still habitually spoken of in the family as Little Fred, notwithstanding that he is a head taller than I, and a strongly built, muscular youth into the bargain. He is in college—a sophomore—and I do not hesitate to declare that when he left school he was about as clean cut a young fellow, both mentally and physically, as anyone would wish to see. I have always encouraged him to take a sensible amount of exercise and have been glad that he seemed fond of the athletic sports in vogue among the growing lads of the country and did not need to be prodded, like his brother David for instance, to keep out of doors. I have been aware that he has been a prominent member of an amateur base-ball nine and foot-ball eleven, and I have been proud to follow in a confused sort of fashion, for the technical terms have changed sadly since I was a boy, the defeats and victories, principally the latter, I think, of those illustrious organizations. Although I was never his equal physically, I look back with considerable pride to my own foot-ball days, and my children have heard me repeatedly describe the famous dash which I once made with the ball from one end of the field to the other, with Tom Ruggs, the butcher's boy, at my heels, and how he never caught me until after I had sent it flying over the goal line, and we had won the game. That was a long time ago now, and we played a very different game, as I have since discovered. I hear a great deal said nowadays about the lack of attention which the older generation gave to manly sports. We did not make much fuss about them, I agree, and consequently some boys may have been allowed to grow to manhood without proper physical training; but it seems to me that most of us were playing something in the fresh air the greater portion of the time. However, I have always been a great believer in manly sports and I wish to continue to be.

When my boy entered college I remember telling him kindly but explicitly that it was a costly matter to send him there, and that I should expect him to make the most of the opportunities for improvement which were offered him. I knew that he was not especially clever at his books like his brother David, yet at the same time I had set him down as a sensible, wide-awake fellow with at least an average amount of brains and with plenty of tact and common sense. It was my hope that he would devote himself to political economy and mathematics, in which case I should try and find an opening for him after graduation with the firm of Leggatt & Paine, our leading bankers. I expected, of course, that he would continue to take a suitable amount of exercise, to keep himself in good trim ; row on the river and not altogether renounce base-ball. Indeed, although I was aware that collegiate sports were a much more serious tax on a student's time than in my day, I should not have seriously demurred had he been selected to row on the University crew or play on the University base-ball nine. I should have greatly preferred to have him steer clear of both ; still, I try to remember that I was once his age myself, and I am given to understand that the rivalry between the several colleges in these matters is more intense than ever. There was a time when nothing seemed to me of such vital interest as whether Harvard or Yale won the boat race. The Darwinian theory paled in comparative importance beside it. Indeed, I still take more interest in it than it deserves, perhaps. Nevertheless, I took pains to impress upon Fred that his studies were to be his first consideration.

We did not play foot-ball in college when I was there, which was the reason, perhaps, why I assumed that it was a boy's game, to be shuffled off with other purely youthful sports when one became a dignified student. I had heard here and there the statement that it was a rough game, which did not impress me very much, recalling as I did my own hacked shins. It was not until I read my friend Horace Plympton's letter to the *Evening Times*, that my attention was particularly called to the matter. Horace seemed to have lashed himself into a perfect fury on the subject. He stigmatized the modern game as it was played by University students as a barbaric spectacle, dangerous to limb, if not to life. Horace has always been more or less of a pepper-pot, but he is not exactly a croaker, and he served in the war with distinction. Hence his diatribe made me frown, even though it rather amused me. It was written in the autumn of the year before Fred went to Cambridge, and I read it aloud to the family circle as being of interest to a sub-freshman.

"What perfect nonsense!" exclaimed that profound young gentleman, when I had finished. "The man who wrote that letter is a flub-dub, father."

Though not aware of the precise meaning of this epithet, I realized that it was a severe arraignment. I felt, too, that my manner of reading the communication had given license to my boy's tongue. I answered, therefore, with some unction:

"The writer, Horace Plympton, is a brave and sensible man. I know him very well."

"I guess he never kicked foot-ball."

"In his day the young men who were fortunate enough to be sent to college were better occupied. Foot-ball? It is a game for high-schools, not universities."

"It is the greatest game of the day, father," said my sub-freshman, with the haughty consciousness of superior knowledge which the waning, though reigning, generation has so often to bow to.

Of course that settled the question. I believe that I made a futile remark to the effect that the president ought to put a stop to it, or something of the sort, but I knew enough to know that I had been convicted of error. I saw Fred glance at his sisters, and all three at their mother, who looked anxious in her desire not to seem to take sides against me, though manifestly sympathizing with them. I said to myself that if foot-ball was the greatest game of the day, I was not going to put my foot down and prevent my boys from playing it merely because I was old fogy enough not to understand that it was the greatest game of the day, and Horace Plympton had written a letter to the *Evening Times*. Accordingly, when the time came for Fred to go to college I merely cautioned him generally against wasting his time, and uttered no fulminations against foot-ball in particular.

"On the University foot-ball eleven?" I echoed, taking the newspaper from my wife, and as I read I felt a little lump of emotional pride rise in my throat. There it was, sure enough, in black and white, though I could not help wondering why the fact was of importance enough to be chronicled in the daily press along with the telegraphic news, and the deaths and marriages. It was evidently a matter of considerable moment, though I could not quite see why.

"He will be perfectly delighted," said Josephine. "He has been extremely doubtful whether he would be chosen. Oh, Fred," she exclaimed, in a tone of solicitude, "do you really think it's safe?"

How exactly that was like a woman. Here was my wife, who had secretly aided and abetted her son in his design, and been the recipient of his hopes and fears on the subject, turning to me, who had dared to utter a feeble protest or two only to be scoffed at, and summarily sat upon, asking if the game was really safe.

"There are certain risks in this world that a man has to take," I answered, borrowing the sentiment which she had uttered on the occasion of our affair with the burglars.

Josephine did not appreciate my irony. "Why, oh why, did you give your consent to his playing foot-ball? she asked, tragically. "I understand that it is a terribly rough and dangerous game."

"I give my consent? This is monstrous, Josephine, monstrous. I did not wish to be a killjoy and a marplot, or I would have forbidden Fred to touch a foot-ball after he entered college. Had you, my dear, given me the least bit of support, I should have nipped the whole business in the bud. Yet now you seek to throw the blame on me."

The suggestion of the dire parental sternness of which I had evidently just missed being guilty caused her thoughts to fly off on an opposite tack. "The poor darling, his heart was so set on being chosen," she said. "I am sure, Fred, it would have been a terrible blow to him if he had not succeeded."

"I dare say that it was his chief motive in going to college," I interjected, a little indignantly.

"I really think it was," she murmured, with sweet maternal sympathy. "I shall live though in constant dread until it is over and done with."

"What is over and done with?"

"The Harvard-Yale foot-ball match. It's on account of that he's been so anxious to belong. And, Fred, he said to me the other day that if he was chosen, he hoped that we would go to Springfield to see the game. It is terrible to think that I might see him killed before my eyes, but he is set on our going."

"It is all a piece of infernal nonsense," I remarked, with majestic dignity; nevertheless, the idea did not strike me as a bad one. To tell the truth, I was beginning to be curious to see this game, which, according to the views of my eldest son, was the greatest game of the day, and to those of Horace Plympton a barbaric spectacle.

And now befell me a curious experience; at least it seemed to me such. I found that I, who, though considered an industrious and painstaking lawyer, have never awakened any especial interest in the community, had acquired lustre and importance by virtue of the circumstance that I had a son on the University foot-ball eleven. College graduates of various ages, who had hitherto classed me with the general run of their acquaintance, grew suddenly cordial and congratulatory in their manner, and I had the satisfaction of reading in the public prints an item to the effect that Frederick ———, the father of the well-known half-back of the Harvard University foot-ball eleven, had recently visited New York for a few days. Altogether I had become, for the first time in my existence, an object of consequence to my fellow-citizens, and almost to the world at large.

As for the hero himself, he bore his importance modestly and meekly, though he evidently considered that he had rescued the family name from obscurity and set it gloriously in the public eye by dint of his renown. He was in strict training, and fiercely conscientious as to what he ate and drank, and as to his hours of sleep. Little was heard in the house when he was at home but conjecture and estimate as to who was likely to win in the impending contest. Had I been properly attentive, I might have learned from his lips not merely the names and nicknames of the members of the respective teams and the positions on the field they were to fill, but their weights in fighting trim, their fine points both as foot-ball kickers and as men, and not improbably their love affairs. When now and then, as occasionally happened, I betrayed by an unfortunate question or by unappreciative silence my lack of familiarity with this or that celebrity, the look of wondering pity with which my boy, and indeed every member of the family, regarded me made me feel myself to be a veritable ignoramus. Josephine and her girls knew the whole business from beginning to end, and I must confess that I secretly drank in more than I pretended.

A fortnight before the match was to come off Sam Bangs, who, as some of you will remember, is a second cousin of mine and rather a pal of Josephine's, appeared at the house one evening and laid before me, in his engaging, plausible fashion, a project which he and his wife and my wife had cooked up between them. He and Josephine assured me, in the first place, that I wouldn't have the least bother in the matter, and that everything would be perfectly plain running for the reason that Sam was intimate with the manager of the railroad, and that little Fred had secured the requisite number of tickets for the game. Then he proceeded to inform me that they had conceived the idea of going to see the game at Springfield in a private special car ; that the manager had promised to let him have one, and that it would be much more jolly to go with a few friends like that and have a luncheon comfortably served by a caterer than to be lumped in the common cars with Tom, Dick, and Harry, who were liable to be noisy students, or still more noisy prize-fighters, and starve ; that there were several people crazy to go whom it would be very pleasant to have, notably Mrs. Guy Sloane and Mrs. Walter Warner (*née* Polly Flinders), and that the expense would be comparatively trifling.

"I think it would be particularly nice, Fred, on Josie's account," added my wife. "I should ask two or three of her girls, and some boys to match. She is inclined to be shy, and this would be just the occasion to help her to feel at her ease with young men. Then I thought you would like to have a chat with Polly Warner ; you so rarely see her now, and you and she used to get on so well together ; and you know Mrs. Guy Sloane always stimulates you. I think you would have a very good time ; and, as Sam says, it's a Dutch treat, so the expense would fall on everybody alike."

Seeing that Josephine's heart was set on going in just that way, I did not attempt to interpose objections. I took the liberty, however, of remarking that, though we as the parents of one of the players had a reason for going, I could not understand why a cultivated woman like Mrs. Guy Sloane was willing, crazy indeed according to what they had said, to take so much trouble to see a pack of college youths knock each other about. In answer to this, Sam declared that every man, woman, and child in the city who could possibly get away was going to Springfield ; that trains were to be run every fifteen minutes, and that no less than twenty special private cars in addition to ours had been chartered for the occasion. Again I hung my diminished head before this broadside of superior information.

Sam was perfectly right. I have rarely seen such a crowd in a small compass as was collected at the railway station before we started. How we ever reached Sam, who made himself visible to me at last across an ocean of heads by lifting himself on the shoulders of obliging friends, and found our special car seems mysterious to me as I look back upon it. It really appeared as though every man, woman, and child in the city *were* going, from the highest officials of the State and our leading citizens in various fields to the veriest street Arab who had managed to beg, borrow, or earn the requisite fare. Everybody, or nearly everybody, carried a flag, and Josephine seemed to think that I, as a Harvard man and the father of the half-back of the team, was lacking in enthusiasm because I had not got possession of one.

"It will be time enough for enthusiasm when we win the match," I remarked, sententiously, though what with the general crowd and the files of students bubbling over with Rah-rah-rahs as they tore along the platform to find seats in the several trains, I was beginning to feel very tremulous about the gills, so to speak.

I doubt if Josephine heard my answer. Her attention had suddenly been absorbed by the sight of Mrs. Willoughby Walton, on the way to her special car, in all her glory, which consisted of a new seal-brown costume with tiger-skin trimmings and a retinue comprising Gillespie Gore, Dr. Henry Meredith, the specialist on nervous diseases (who, like everybody else, had evidently taken a day off), and half a dozen youths who looked young enough to be freshmen. She was frantically waving a crimson flag, which she shook at the windows of our car as she passed with the spirit of a belle of nineteen.

" That woman is simply wonderful," murmured my darling. " She is fifty-five if she is a day, but she will not give up."

" Rah ! rah ! rah ! Harvard ! " I ejaculated hysterically. I felt that I was getting rattled, as my famous son calls it.

" Look here, Cousin Fred," said Sam Bangs at my shoulder. " Seen the morning paper ? Here he is cabinet size and a full family history annexed. It's something which his great-grandchildren will be proud of. Where the dickens, by the way, is Mrs. Sloane? I've been looking for her everywhere in the station. She's coming, because she telephoned me last night to inquire if I could squeeze one more into our car. We'll be off in another five minutes."

"What *do* you mean, Sam? What is it?" asked Josephine, as she seized and held to the light the newspaper which he was extending.

I looked over her shoulder and broke into a cold perspiration at beholding an execrable three-quarters length cut of my darling son superscribed by his name in holograph.

"It's an indecent outrage," I hissed.

"It isn't like him in the least. No one would ever know who it was. It makes him look like a prize-fighter," cried Josephine.

"They've no right to print his picture at all; it'll do the boy a serious injury by leading him to believe there is nothing else in the world worth thinking about but foot-ball," I asserted. "What right have they to do it?"

"Pooh, Cousin Fred," said Sam. "It's

nothing but ordinary newspaper enterprise. They print everybody's portrait nowadays, from the common murderer up. Your ox is gored this time, that's all. Cheer up, old man—Rah ! rah ! rah ! Harvard !"

" I never supposed they would make him look like that, or I wouldn't have let Fred have the photograph to give them," said Josephine, forlornly.

"Do you mean that you gave it to them?" I asked, in horror.

" It was to Fred I gave it. He said that his picture was to appear with the others, and that he must have a photograph. But they have made him much the worst looking of them all. It's a libel on the dear boy."

I was saved from intemperate language by the sudden advent of Mrs. Guy Sloane, in whose custody appeared the Rev. Bradley Mason, our spiritual adviser. They were both breathless with haste, occasioned, as we shortly learned, by the necessity imposed on our beloved pastor of marrying a couple before he could escape from his fold.

" If I had ever dreamed that you would

come, Mr. Mason, I should have sent you an invitation myself," said Josephine, whose delight, as I perceived, was tinged with jealousy.

"I planned it as a delicious surprise," interjected Mrs. Sloane. "I knew you would be only too glad to have him if there was room. I dare say you thought I was a little mysterious over the telephone last night, Mr. Bangs," she added with a blithe twist of her neck in Sam's direction.

"I am a thorough believer in the efficacy of manly sports on character," I heard Mr. Mason remark to my wife. "They cannot be too much encouraged by us all."

"It is very kind of you to say so," said Josephine, with a radiance which told me plainly that her qualms concerning the whole proceeding as an educational factor were at least temporarily dispelled. "I shall tell little Fred that you were with us. It will gratify him very much to know that you saw the game."

"It must be a proud day for you as a father and a college man," he continued, with a kindly smile in my direction.

"Really, sir, I am not altogether certain yet," I answered, a trifle doggedly. "My judgment is in a state of suspension."

He obviously mistook my philosophic utterance for fears concerning the outcome of the game, inasmuch as he presently sought to soothe me by a speech to the effect that a game well lost was a victory in ethics, which prompted me to remark, under my breath:

"Provided it doesn't cost a leg or a rib or two."

"Cost nothing," cried the irrepressible Sam, whose ear caught what I had meant for an aside. "He'll come out of it all right, Cousin Fred. We're bound to win too. Rah! rah! rah! Harv-a-rd!" Thereupon the engine gave a puff and a couple of snorts, and we were off.

V

WE were early on the ground. That is to say, only a few hundred people were in their places when we arrived. The seating accommodations were for thousands. Have you ever seen an intercollegiate foot-ball field? If not, picture to yourself a long, level, rectangular arena about a hundred yards long and fifty yards wide marked out with white lines at certain regular intervals. At either end stands a crossbar supported by two posts. These are the respective goals. All along the field on either side runs a tall tier of seats similar to those at a hippodrome, and there are tiers of seats also opposite the ends ; but the best seats are likely to be those on either side in proximity to the middle of the field.

Sam Bangs led the way with the confident tread of a drum-major down the Harvard side —for the custom is to apportion the seats on one of the long sides of the field among the friends of one college, and those on the other correspondingly—until he reached a desirable location. Then we established ourselves according to his directions and waited. It was rather a long wait—nearly two hours—during which I had ample leisure to philosophize to the top of my bent. We had to console us Sam's assurance that it was necessary to take time by the forelock to this radical extent in order to secure satisfactory places. For the next two hours a steady stream of people poured along the two sides of the field until they became great walls of crimson and blue humanity. Flags waved, badges fluttered, the human voice worked itself hoarse in every form of encouraging outcry from the full-chested song to the indiscriminate cat-call. In front of each section of seats stood a separate youth, who at very short intervals, and at the slightest provacation, invoked cheers upon cheers for everything and everybody, from the captain of the team to the college coster-monger. An hour before the game began the benches were crowded, and I seemed to have recognized in the passing throng every person of consideration among my acquaintance. Mrs. Willoughby Walton and her party were among the last to arrive. I was curious to see where they would bestow themselves, seeing that we were all packed tight as herrings, and there was only here and there an occasional chance for another mortal to squeeze in, and that generally at the cost of clambering over the heads of two or three hundred people. As Josephine said to me later, I might have known that Mrs. Walton would not put herself in any such plight. I was just wondering what on earth her elegant procession, which had halted in front of the section next to ours, was going to do, when of a sudden the occupants of the two best rows of seats trooped out in orderly file and relinquished their places to the fashionable party. Sam, after a moment's dazed silence, which must have been gall to him, for he does not like to be imposed upon in such matters, furnished us with the solution of this act of legerdemain.

"They were mill hands subsidized to come early and hold the seats until Mrs. Willoughby arrived.

Another hour of anticipation, and then at last a roar ; a roar which runs like a fire down our side of the field, waking tired lungs to new enthusiasm and calling into action every crimson flag and rag. Only the wearers of the blue are quiet ; their benches remain coldly silent. The Harvard eleven have arrived on a tally-ho, and in a few minutes more are disporting themselves like a band of prairie dogs over the campus. The uproar is deafening, but they seem to pay no attention to it. They strip off their crimson jerseys and concentrate their energies on bunting and punting a leather foot-ball about the field. They wear earth-colored canvas jackets and earth-colored knickerbockers ending in crimson stockings, and I say to myself that they are the most unpleasant-looking band of ruffians I have ever beheld. Nor are my fond paternal eyes able to make a reservation in little Fred's favor on this point. I have considerable difficulty, indeed, in distinguishing him from his mates, though Josephine declares that she singled him out the moment he appeared on the scene. He suggests to me a compromise between a convict and a hod-carrier. Nevertheless, my eyes begin to water as I follow his every movement, and my pulses throb eagerly. At the same time I am impelled to link my arm affectionately in my son David's, next to whom I am sitting. I cannot help wondering what he, dear boy, is thinking of it all. He is perfectly healthy, but he is slight, and will never be an athlete. His tastes do not run in that direction. He graduated at school last summer next to the head of his class, and it was no class of two, but of twenty times that number. We were very proud of it, Josephine and I. We went to the exhibition and saw him receive a number of prizes. It was a pleasant occasion, but how trifling and insignificant were the plaudits he received compared with the uproarious ovation accorded a successful halfback. I feel almost indignant, even in the midst of my excitement over little Fred, and would fain throw my arms round his brother's neck and whisper that he must not take the matter to heart, and that the whole business is terribly unjust.

Now comes another uproar, and this time from the opposite side of the field. The Yale eleven have arrived and are stripping off their jerseys. They career over the arena in dirt color and dark blue, while the dark blue benches surge tumultuously. There is no more delay. The umpire calls the game, and the two sides line up for action. I feel Josephine, who is on my other side, clutch my arm and sigh. There is only one object for her on the field, as I well know. She has been trying to learn the rules from Sam for the last half hour (she doubts my knowledge on such subjects nowadays), and I can see that she is seeking in vain to concentrate her mind on her new-found information and to shut out the vision of little Fred being borne off the field on a litter. I confess that Horace Plympton's letter recurs to me for a moment, but I shake myself and utter an inward "Pooh!" and haughtily determine to view the contest dispassionately and from the standpoint of a third person and a philosopher.

Harvard has won the toss and is to have the ball. In my day we had to kick it ; now it is manipulated with the hands, and not forward, but backward. The players form a phalanx, and one of their number snaps, as it is called, the ball between his legs to someone behind him, who in turn passes it to another, who is expected to make a forward dash with it. Before I can quite realize what is being done the Harvard men are speeding toward the Yale goal in a V-shaped body. Little Fred has the ball. Or rather he had it. All I can see now is an indiscriminate mass of bodies, legs, and arms. A great pile of men are struggling on the ground, and I have reason to believe that little Fred is at the bottom of the pile.

"A scrimmage," says Sam, looking round at Josephine.

"Oh, yes," she answers, with apparent calm, but I can feel her tremble.

"This is nothing ; it's like this most of

the time," says Sam. "You see he's all right, and——"

A yell cuts him short.

"Good enough! Harvard still has the ball," he continues, at its close.

"Can you see him?" whispers Josephine in my ear.

"He's all right," I murmur, assuringly.

See him! I can see him distinctly. He has lost his cap already; his hair is in wild confusion; he is covered with dirt from head to foot; he limps a little. But Harvard still has the ball. And Sam says it is nothing and like this most of the time. Sam must know.

"Rah! rah! rah! Harvard!" I cry with the rest unflinchingly.

There is a second yell, this time from our enemies. Harvard has lost the ball and Yale has it. And now before my bewildered eyes scrimmage follows scrimmage with fierce iteration, and one pile of bodies, arms, and legs succeeds another. The player, fortunate enough to carry or force the ball a yard or more toward the rival goal by a frantic rush before he is overwhelmed and squashed, reaps a whirlwind of applause from the absorbed multitude. Every inch of ground is disputed. Once in a long interval when the ball gets dangerously near a goal, someone on the imperiled side kicks it half the length of the field, and the scrimmages are renewed. But it is rarely kicked at all except at such junctures. Foot-ball! I say to myself that it is a gladiatorial combat with an occasional punt thrown in by way of identification. But every one around me is declaring that the play of both sides is magnificent, that the team work is perfection, and the head qualities displayed unique in the annals of the game. Sam tells me again and again that Fred is doing sheer wonders and is the backbone of the Harvard side, and I wonder how he can distinguish so easily which is Fred and whether he has any backbone left. I can no longer make out much of anything except that one ruffian closely resembles every other ruffian, and that one poor boy is lying on the ground perfectly still, as though he were dead. There is just a little lull on the benches. People are interested.

"Who is it?" gasps Josephine. "Is it he, dear?"

"Butchered to make a Roman holiday," I mutter between my teeth, with my heart in my mouth.

They are pulling and rubbing the victim, and a doctor, retained for such emergencies, is bending over him. After a few moments more he rises slowly, looks round him in a dazed fashion, and resumes his position with a painful limp, to a round of applause.

"It isn't Fred," says Josephine.

"But he has a mother, though," I answer.

"He'll be all right in a minute or two," says Sam. "They stamped the wind out of him, that's all."

To have the wind stamped out of one is a mere bagatelle, of course, and I have forgotten it in another moment under the spur of excitement. A Harvard player has the ball, and no one seems to be able to stop him. He throws off his antagonist and dodges two others, and races down the field like a deer, while the wearers of the crimson scream his name with transport and flourish their banners like madmen. It is Fred, it is Fred, it is Fred! I know his figure now. He has the ball and is flying like the wind with two great brutes at his heels. Will they catch him? Will they kill him? They are gaining on him.

"Run—run—run," I shout, in spite of myself, while all the people on our benches rise in their excitement, and Josephine covers her eyes with her hands, unwilling to look. On, on my boy runs, until at last he falls with his two pursuers on top of him full across the Yale line.

"A touch-down, a touch-down!" bursts out Sam, as he grasps my hand in his wild enthusiasm. I do not know exactly what has occurred except that there is pandemonium on the Harvard side of the field unequalled as yet by anything that has happened, and a deathly tranquility along the benches opposite. After making sure that Fred is still alive, I listen to the explanation that a touch-down counts a certain number of points, and gives the right to the side which wins it to try to kick a goal. This attempt is presently made. A player lies on the ground and holds the ball between his hands for another to kick. Presto ! the ball sails through the air ; for an instant there is agonized suspense, and then a shout from Yale. It has failed to go between the goal-posts, and consequently has missed.

"Four to nothing, anyway," says Sam. "That was a magnificent run. Rah ! rah ! rah ! Harvard."

Josephine is wiping her eyes and everybody in our neighborhood is nudging each other in consequence of the news that we are blood relations of the hero of the hour. Mrs. Sloane nods her congratulations, and Mrs. Walton signals with a crimson flag from the adjoining section, and our beloved pastor smiles at Josephine in his delightful way.

And what follows ? What follows is fierce and harrowing. What follows continues to hold that great audience spellbound to the close. The score is four to nothing in favor of Harvard; but the Yale team, smarting from defeat, throw themselves into the ever-recurring scrimmages with set faces. It is not my purpose to follow the contest in detail. I am writing as a father and philosopher, and not as a chronicler of athletic struggles. Suffice it to state that the scrimmages grow still more savage and earnest, and that a player from each side is obliged by the referee to retire from the field, because he has slugged an opponent. Suffice it to state that presently a rusher is obliged to retire from the field by reason of a sprained ankle. It is not little Fred, but might it not have been? Suffice it to state that by the end of the first three-quarters of an hour—let the uninitiated here learn that a match is divided into two bouts of that length each, with an interim of fifteen minutes—the Yale team, by the most magnificent work (according to Sam Bangs), has forced the ball steadily and surely toward the Harvard line, and won a touch-down and kicked a goal, leaving the score for the first half six to four in favor of the blue. Just after the ball has flown between the goal-posts, amid thunders of triumph from our enemies, the umpire calls time.

Suffice it to state that the second three-quarters of an hour is largely a repetition of the first—short, furious rushes, everlasting scrimmages, and here and there a punt. The ruffians look still more ruffianly from frequent contact with mother-earth and the clutches of one another. Ominous gloom and depressing silence take possession of the friends of Harvard; their very cheers are anxious, and with good reason. Yale has kicked another goal from the field in the first twenty minutes and the crimson is being gradually and steadily outplayed. My heart bleeds for my son; he will be so disappointed if he loses. And I shall be so happy when the game is over and I am sure that he is not maimed for life. He is doing wonders still, dear boy. Twice I see him lying flat and motionless on the field with the wind stamped out of him, to borrow Sam's euphemism, while his mother wriggles in her seat in the throes of uncertainty and is hardly to be restrained from going to him. Twice, after the doctor has fumbled over him and water has been dashed in his face, I see Sam's diagnosis vindicated, and my half-back rise to his feet, and the game go on as though nothing had happened. Such episodes are a matter of course, and not to be taken too seriously. A broken rib or two is not a vital matter, and only one rib is broken in the second three-quarters of an hour. Even then the poor victim does not have to be carried off on a litter, for he is able to walk with the help of the doctor and a friend. It is not Fred : Fred has merely had the wind stamped out of him a few times and is still doing wonders. Will it never end? I look at my watch feverishly. The ball is close by the Harvard goal, and Yale holds it there with the tenacity of a bull-dog. Bull-dog? They are all bull-dogs—twenty-two bull-dogs cheek by jowl.

"Isn't it magnificent?" murmurs Sam, looking back at me. "They have outplayed us fairly and squarely. Only five minutes left, and the score eleven to four against us. We're not in it. That run of Fred's was the most brilliant play of the day, though."

"The poor darling will be broken-hearted," whispers Josephine.

"That is better than being broken-headed—better for us," I whisper in reply.

"I do hope he hasn't lost any of his front

teeth. His mouth was bleeding the last time he fell," continues his mother.

"False ones nowadays are very satisfactory," I answer.

Ten minutes later we are moving along with the rest of our acquaintance on the way to the railroad. Yale has won, eleven to four, and the bruised and battered players of both teams have departed on their respective tally-hos, and Josephine and I are free to receive the congratulations of our friends with a calm mind, though my darling is still haunted by the fear that our illustrious son has left a tooth or two on the arena. Fred's run is on everybody's lips, and we as the authors of his being are made much of. Mr. Leggatt, the banker, works his way up to me through the crowd at great personal distress, for he is a fat man, in order to say, with an enthusiastic shake of the hand :

"Great boy that of yours; splendid grit; I must have him when he graduates."

I sputter many thanks confusedly. Here is a strange development truly. I had been hoping, as you may remember, to be able to go to Mr. Leggatt, at Fred's graduation, and to ask for a clerkship for my boy on the plea of his steadiness and sterling common sense ; and now the solicitation has come to me on the score of his grit as a foot-ball kicker. The world seems just a little topsy-turvy, and I am not quite sure whether to laugh or to cry.

We got home at last somehow ; and here I am sitting in my library trying to collect my faculties and to appreciate the honor which has been thrust upon me—the honor of being the father of a famous half-back. To tell the truth, it sticks in my crop just a little and does not relish to the extent which would seem appropriate. Indeed I am not altogether sure whether I can see a distinction between being the father of a famous half-back and the father of a famous toreador or famous prize-fighter. I know that Leggatt and one or two others, to whom I ventured to expose my qualms on the way home, declared them preposterous, and that the game was magnificent discipline for both mind and body. Come to that, the vicissitudes of a matador are magnificent discipline for both mind and body. So are those of a gladiator. Yet I have my doubts whether Leggatt would like to be the father of either. Nevertheless, although he is a citizen of far greater consideration than I, he gave me to understand that he would be proud to be described in the newspapers as the father of a famous half-back, and to see a son of his handed down to posterity in the public prints as a prize animal of this description.

I fear there must be a screw loose somewhere in my make-up as a father and a philosopher. You remember the case of the burglars? It did not seem to me worth while to go downstairs and expose myself to be shot. Yet Josephine felt differently on the point.

Moreover, I have never been able to understand why it is courageous or meritorious to be an amateur Alpine climber, whereas many are fain to admire the beauties of nature from an elevation where a false step or a rotten rope would be passports to destruction. Then, again, people who cross the ocean in dories, or fast for indefinite periods, have never aroused my enthusiasm. On the contrary, I regard them as being in the same general category with lunatics. I have never seen a bull-fight, and I have sometimes fancied that I should be weak enough to attend one out of curiosity if I happened to be in Spain at the right time ; but I am sure that I should never care to go twice. And yet I am expected to feel proud and grateful because my eldest son has made prowess at foot-ball the aim and object of his college course. I am trying to, trying hard, but I fear it is no use. I should like to understand why it is glorious or sensible for an honest, strapping fellow, who has been sent to college by dint of some economy on the part of his parents, to devote his entire energies to a course of training which will entitle him to run the risk of having his legs, arms, or ribs broken in fighting for a leather ball before several thousand people. Of one thing I am certain already, even at the risk of seeming to agree with Horace Plympton, which is, that if I had another son with like proclivities, I should put a stop to it.

But then, as Josephine reminds me, the fact

that our David does not care a picayune for anything of the sort, robs my resolve of much of its solemnity. I might, to be sure, interpose a mandate at this late hour and cut off little Fred in the flower of his renown, and (to quote my wife once more) break his heart; which might be a more serious consequence than a broken leg. No, I am inclined to think, on the whole, now that the mischief is done, we may as well let him follow the path he has chosen, especially as Leggatt has his eye on him and has promised to give him a start. We must live in the hope that the breath will not be trampled out of him once too often before that desirable result is brought to pass. Moreover, if he is borne of the field on a litter, it will not be in the presence of his parents. We have seen one gladiatorial combat, and our thirst for gore is sated.

Henceforth we shall be content to cower by the hearth on the days when the great matches are played and fancy each ring at the door-bell the summons of a telegraphic emissary. And by way of celebrating our first escape from bereavement, I am going to present our David with a gold watch for the excellent showing he made in his studies last summer.

VI

LITTLE FRED has been graduated from college without the loss of his front teeth or an eye. He has a few scars, which will not permanently disfigure him ; and though he halts slightly as the result of a strained tendon in the calf of one of his legs, Dr. Meredith assures us that this is chiefly a nervous symptom, which will pass off presently. He says Fred is a little run down, and he advises raw eggs and milk between meals. I assume that the doctor is right, but it seems strange to me that a boy should get run down through foot-ball exercise. However, he is to go abroad for six months, which ought to mend matters, and then buckle down to work with Leggatt & Paine. He is an honest, manly fellow, who will make friends, and, provided he does not break his neck in following the hounds or playing polo, is likely to do well.

David, my second boy, is a born chemist and a genuine book-lover besides. He is at the School of Science, to which we decided to send him, instead of to college, in view of the fact that his proclivities were in the line of gases and forces rather than Greek roots and history. He is doing famously, I believe; and though I am a profound ignoramus on such matters, I should not be at all surprised if he were to make a name for himself early in life by some valuable discovery in the electrical or bacillic line. He has lately made a test of all the wall-papers and upholstery in our house, and discovered, to our dismay, that there is arsenic in pretty nearly everything, including some of the bed-sheets, which, strange to state, in spite of their innocent appearance, proved to be particularly full of the deleterious poison. We have had to overhaul everything in consequence, and Josephine firmly believes that Fred's nervous halt is due to the presence of arsenic in his system, for the bed-sheets in his college room belonged to the condemned batch. Seeing that the rest of us are perfectly well, I secretly suspect that late hours and tobacco are more to blame than arsenic for my athletic son's condition; but in the teeth of scientific warning I have not ventured to run the risk of continued exposure, and have consented to the purchase of new carpets, curtains, window-shades, and other household apparel.

I am much more concerned, to tell the truth, lest some of the germs which David is cosseting in his bed-chamber may get loose and ravage the community. He has a bacillus farm, where, according to his account, the cholera germ, the germ of tuberculosis, the typhoid-fever germ, and the diphtheria germ are growing side by side for his private edification. As Josephine says, there are certain risks which a brave man has to take; but I am not sure that this is one of them. Even my darling is a little anxious on the score of contamination, in spite of her scientific son's assurance that his pets are thoroughly harmless.

I do not really know whether Josephine is prouder of Fred or of David. Certainly her mind is comparatively at rest regarding them both, notwithstanding my second boy is not quite like other people. I do not mean that he is boorish or eccentric, merely that he is bookish and self-absorbed. He takes no interest in his personal appearance, and he avoids every young woman except his sisters. Fred is dandified, keenly fond of the social interests of the day and of the other sex. I foresee that he bids fair to be a leading man of affairs, and to figure prominently in society, and later on to become a member of Congress or to be sent abroad as a foreign minister. But he is just like everybody else, so to speak; or rather he accepts the world as he finds it and accommodates himself to it. Now, David is cast in a different mould. He is essentially unconventional. And yet, though his mother sighs now and then over his repugnance to young ladies, and tries to badger him into looking a little more spruce, I can perceive that she is thoroughly proud of his originality and independence, and believes that he is even more likely than his conventional brother to distinguish himself and immortalize the family name. Josephine used to say, when the boys were little, that she hoped one of them would be a clergyman, and I know that she has more sympathy than I—and I have considerable—with a scheme of life which entertains starving in a garret for the sake of art or science as a meritorious contingency. She has held up before her boys, since their earliest childhood, the perils of idle and purely worldly living, and spurred them to make the most of themselves.

Curiously enough, our two girls are just as dissimilar to each other as Fred and David. Josie, the elder—who, as I have already specified, is, according to the world at large, the image of her mother at the same age—will not be troublesome in the least degree, so my wife tells me. She has taken to society as a duck takes to water. She has a natural aptitude for pleasing and being pleased; consequently she has plenty of partners. My wife says that, considering the dear child was all legs and arms three years ago, we have every reason to congratulate ourselves that she has turned out such a pleasant-looking girl, and that her red hair is decidedly ornamental. I call her handsome, but Josephine declares that I make myself ridiculous by the assertion, and that it is very rare that a girl who has not really a ray of beauty to commend her becomes such a thorough-going favorite in her first season.

"She constantly reminds me of you, and that is enough for me," I remarked, tenderly, on one occasion.

"You make me boil when you say that, Fred. I was really a very pretty girl, if I do say it; whereas Josie, the sweet soul, only just escapes being homely. Her smile and her hair save her, so that she passes. But it is a libel to compare her with what I was at her age. We must look facts in the face, dear."

"People tell me every day that she is the living image of her mother," I answered humbly.

"People are idiots. They know you will believe it because you are a man. They don't dare tell me anything of the sort. No, Fred, we must build all our hopes of beauty on Winona."

" Ah ! " I remarked, with an intonation of pride ; even her mother will not be able to pick a flaw in *her*."

" She is a very handsome girl, but———"

Josephine stopped short, and I could see that her lip was trembling with emotion.

" There is no ' but,' " I protested. " Whatever Josie may be, Winona is a raving beauty."

" Oh, yes, Fred, I am perfectly satisfied with her looks. That makes it all the harder. I'm on tenterhooks lest she is going to be queer."

" Queer ? " I inquired, with agitation, dreading some disclosure of mental derangement.

" Odd—not like other people. It would break my heart, Fred. She is seventeen, and she doesn't take the slightest interest in coming out. You remember I had her appear for an hour at Josie's party, and that she was surrounded by young men from the moment she entered the room until I sent her to bed? Most girls would have been in danger of having their heads turned. Winona was bored."

"She will get over that as soon as she is a year older. She is shy."

"She is not shy. If she were shy I should think nothing of it. She declares that society is all nonsense, and that she wishes never to come out at all."

"What an egregiously sensible girl," I murmured.

"I hope you will not encourage her, Fred," pleaded my darling. "I have counted so much on her. If Josie had taken it into her head to be queer, I shouldn't have said a word, for I think myself that is often for a plain girl's happiness not to have to undergo the ordeal of being neglected ; but in the case of a beauty like Winona it would be such a waste! There is not a girl of her age who compares with her in beauty."

"What is it she wishes to do?" I asked, with a knitted brow. A man is apt to leave the management of his own daughters to his wife, even though he is a philosopher and prolific in theories. I had rather taken it for granted that certain advanced notions of mine regarding the conduct of women's lives would be allowed to lie dormant in my brain for lack of an animating cause, or, more accurately speaking, for lack of moral courage on my part to exploit them for the benefit of my own flesh and blood. It is more satisfactory to try experiments in the line of education on some one else's children. Besides, I had argued that Josephine was the proper person to propose a departure from the established method, in conformity with which conclusion I had paid out a handsome round sum for a coming-out party and a social wardrobe for my eldest girl. But now I felt in conscience bound to prick up my ears.

"She doesn't know herself what she wishes to do," said my wife, dejectedly. "She is daft on the subject of books and education."

"Is not that rather to her credit?" I ventured to inquire.

Josephine gazed at me as though my words had stung her.

"Of course it is to her credit," she replied, almost fiercely. "You know perfectly well, Fred, I have encouraged the girls to study and cultivate their minds in every conceivable manner, and that I have always said they should have equal advantages in the way of education with their brothers so far as it was possible to procure them. I have just told you that if Josie had wished to be a student and to go in for a career of some kind, I should have been perfectly willing; yes, I should have been glad. But it does seem hard that they should change places, and the one who is a radiant beauty, and sure to be universally admired, should take it into her head to cut loose from society. I remember saying when she was christened that we were gambling with Divine Providence in giving her such an individualizing name, for fear she would grow up a fright. I little thought I was running the risk of such a contingency as this."

"It *is* hard, Josephine," I murmured, wishing to be sympathetic. "I think, though, you are a little premature in taking it for granted that Winona will not come round all right in the end."

My darling shook her head. "She may consent to go about in order to please me, but her heart will never be in it. Oh, I know!" she added, with another outburst, as though she were arguing with an accusing spirit, "that society is all very frivolous in theory and a waste of time, and that the moralists and people who never had the chance to go anywhere would tell me I ought to be thankful to have a daughter who cares for something besides going to balls and dinner-parties and flirting with young men. That's the way they would look at it; but they might argue until they were black in the face and they couldn't make me feel otherwise than disappointed. And, what is more, I believe that Winona will be very sorry herself ten years hence if she perseveres in her present determination."

These last words were spoken by my wife almost tragically, and it was evident to me that they proceeded from the heart. I am free to confess that when Josephine gives utterance to opinions with so much earnestness as this I cannot help feeling that there must be more or less truth in them. She may be no philosopher, but she is a sensible woman.

And especially in a matter where another woman, and one of her own flesh and blood, besides, is concerned, it would certainly seem as though she would be apt to be right. This whole business of the emancipation of woman is one well adapted to drive a philosopher, to say nothing of the father of a family, crazy. Naturally I wish my daughters to become all that they ought to be. On the other hand, if a paterfamilias cannot trust his better half on this particular subject, he may as well imitate the example of certain savage tribes, and make mince-meat of the girls. Perhaps I seem to be worked up on the subject? Well, I am. The din of the moralists, and of the people who have never had a chance to go anywhere, is in my ears, and I cannot get altogether rid of it. Let us start afresh and attack the question from another point of view.

There is no doubt, even to the average masculine mind, although the possessor of the mind may not publish the fact on the housetops, that the most interesting product of this enlightened century is emancipated woman. There are certain enthusiasts, though principally of the emancipated sex, who are already so confident as to the rapid future progress and ultimate glorious evolution of womankind that they are ready to venture the prediction to people whom they think they can trust, that sooner or later there will be no more men. Whether this desirable result is to be brought about by the gradual extinction or snuffing out of the hitherto sterner sex by a process of killing kindness, or by the discovery of a system of generation whereby women only will be procreated, is not foretold by these seers of the future ; accordingly, while one might not be warranted in dismissing the theory as untenable, its fulfilment may fairly be regarded as a remote expectancy, and consigned to the consideration of real philosophers.

There is no doubt, though, that woman has been kept down for generations, and has only just begun to bob up serenely, to hazard a coloquial metaphor. The eyes of civilization are upon her, and there is legitimate curiosity from Christiania to Yokohama to discover what she is going to do. To me as a philosopher, and taking into account one consideration with another, including Josephine's plaint, it seems as though woman would have much plainer sailing in her progress toward reconstruction if it were not that she is so exceedingly good-looking in spots and bunches. Let her distinction as an ornamental factor be totally negatived and overcome, and there is no telling how rapidly she might progress. By ornament, I mean, of course, not merely beauty of face and form, but sweetness of speech, delicacy of physique and sentiment, captivating clothes, and all those distinguishing characteristics which have tended to fasten upon the female sex the epithet of gentle. It will generally be admitted that women of homely presence, clumsy in their gait, dowdy in their dress, and raucous in their intonation, are much safer from the infliction of gallantries at the hands or lips of mortal men than those whose attributes are more pleasing; and it is safe to assert that many a male monster has been rooted to his seat in street-cars by the coldly intellectual eye of some not altogether ablebodied feminine person. The recent victories all along the line of women over men in examination-rooms, and their more or less successful ventures in the fields of law, medicine, and newspaper enterprise, would be more appalling to man and encouraging to the progressionists, but for the obstinate though obvious adhesion of the great mass of womankind to the trick bequeathed to them by their great-great-grandmothers of trying to look as well as they can. And the terrible part of it is they succeed so wonderfully that philosophers like myself are apt to find our ratiocinations wofully mixed when we try to reason about the matter.

You remember, perhaps, that Josephine induced me earlier in our wedded life to give a large party for her sister Julia? Within a year I have submitted to a similar domestic upheaval on account of my elder daughter, and I do not think that it can be said that I acquitted myself in either case malignantly or even morosely. Indeed, though this is not strictly relevant to the discussion, my wife informed me after Josie's party was over that I had behaved like an angel. Now, my sister-in-law, Julia, is still unmarried, and she cannot be far from thirty. As I reflected at the time she came out, she is less comely than my wife and not so sagacious, but she is decidedly an attractive girl. She has had every advantage in the line of social entertainments, and every opportunity to meet available young men. She has waltzed all winter and been successively to Bar Harbor and Newport in summer. She has been to Europe so as to let people forget her and to reappear as a novelty, and she has altered the shape of her hair twice to my individual observation. Yet somehow she hangs fire. I am informed by Josephine, in strict confidence, that she has had offers and might have been married to at least one eminently desirable man before this had she seen fit to accept him ; but I tell my darling that though the consciousness of what might have been may be a legitimate consolation to her and to her sister, it does not controvert the bald fact that Julia is still unmarried at the end of ten years of social divagations.

I do not mean that Julia may not marry.

Very likely she will. She certainly ought to if she has the desire; and she has time enough yet if the right man only thinks so. It is rather on the system I am pondering than on the individual, though the vision of Josie at thirty unwedded, and a little hard and worn, haunts my retina and makes me feel philosophical. Away down in the bottom of my boots or my soul, or wherever a man can most safely harbor a secret reflection, has long lain a feeling of wonder that the world continues to put its daintiest, most cherished, and most carefully tended daughters through the peculiar social programme in vogue. Is it not bewilderingly true that every young woman of position and manners in Christendom, be her father a Knight of the Garter or a Congressman, her mother an azure-blooded countess or the ambitious better half of a retired grocer, finds on the threshold of life only one course open to her if she desires to be conventional, and to do what is naturally expected of her? From twelve to eighteen instruction—and in these latter days exemplary instruction—Latin, Greek, if there is a craving for it, history, psychology, chemistry, political economy, to say nothing of the modern languages and special courses in summer in botany, conchology, and physiology. And then, dating from a long anticipated day, or rather night, a metamorphosis startling as the transition of the cocoon; a formal letting loose of the finished maiden on the polished parquet floor of the social arena. Tra-la-la-la-la! Tra-la-la-la-la! Off she whirls to the rythm of a Strauss waltz or a blood-stirring polka, and for the next four years, on an average, she never stops, metaphorically speaking. She may not always be waltzing or polkaing, but if she is conventionally sound she is sure to be in a whirl. She exchanges daylight for gaslight; her daily sustenance is stewed mushrooms with a rich gray gravy, beef-tea, and ice-cream, varied by an occasional mouthful of fillet as a conscience composer. All winter she participates in a feverish round of balls, receptions, luncheons, dinners, teas, theatre parties, with every now and then a wedding. All summer she sails, floats, glides, sits, perches, sprawls, walks, meanders, talks, climbs, rides, saunters, or dances madly as her mood or circumstances suggest. There is her life, varying a little according to clime and disposition, according to whether she is daughter of a duke or of a successful grocer. It is what everyone expects of her, so no one is surprised ; and she is expected also to keep up the pace until she is married, which is likely to come to pass any day, but which, as in the case of poor Julia, may not be until she is thirty. Fancy living on mushrooms with a rich gray gravy and successively waltzing, meandering, or floating with the Tom, Dick, and Harry of the workaday social world from eighteen to thirty ! And yet we fathers and philosophers ask ourselves why in thunder (or even more vehemently) our daughters have nervous prostration. Why should they? And yet I hear Josephine ask, for the discussion is uppermost in our thoughts at the moment :

"Do you wish Winona to become a second Miss Jacket?"

Let me explain that Miss Jacket, Miss Cora Jacket, M.D., lives opposite to us, and has for some months been a serious menace to the happiness of Josephine, in that my wife declares that the wretch is poisoning our Winona's mind. The charge startled me seriously when it was broached, but I have been trying to consider dispassionately whether the injury likely to be worked will be greater than that consequent upon a continuous fare of mushrooms with rich gray gravy and flirtation. Winona and Miss Cora Jacket, M.D., are certainly thicker than thieves; hence a pardonable lurking suspicion in Josephine's mind that the older woman is seeking to induce the beauty of our family to study medicine. Dr. Jacket must be thirty—just about the age of my sister-in-law. To me she appears to be a trig, energetic little woman, rather pretty and rather well dressed, and though she seems intelligent there is nothing especially frigid or forbidding in her eye. Its intellectuality is not forced upon one. I have found her so attractive that I ventured to insinuate, by way of answer to my wife's expostulation, that Winona might do much worse than model herself on Miss Cora Jacket, M.D. This drew upon my head the vial of Josephine's righteous wrath.

"Now, Fred, just stop and think for one moment," she said. "I have not a word to say against Miss Jacket. I have no doubt she is a most worthy young woman and an excellent physician, though I should never care to consult her myself. But that is neither here nor there. Do you happen to know what Miss Jacket's antecedents were, and what her life has been?"

I shook my head droopingly.

"She was born in Ohio, and was left an orphan, and practically unprovided for, at an early age. She was helped by kind friends— all this is from her own lips—until she was old enough to help herself by teaching, and then, by some means or other, she came East and studied medicine, and made the start for herself that you see. All of which, I beg to anticipate you in saying, is marvellously to her credit. She is plainly a brilliant and capable young woman of whom any mother might be proud, provided she had to be. But because it was creditable and sensible in Miss Jacket to make the most of herself in that particular way, you surely would not advocate that the daughters of the Princess of Wales and the Empress of Germany should do the same."

"I should certainly advocate their doing something useful," I said in my dogged fashion. "Besides, Winona is the daughter neither of the Princess of Wales nor the Empress of Germany."

"No, she is not," said Josephine, in a tone which seemed to imply that she was grateful for the escape. After all, who of us to-day would give a rush to be a king or queen? What successful business or professional man would exchange the exquisite comfort of the domestic hearth and all the magazines for the prerogatives of royalty? I understand perfectly what Josephine wished to express, and agreed with her on the point. Her daughters, save for a little pomp and circumstance, were practically the peers of any and all princesses.

"Just consider, for a moment, Winona and Miss Jacket side by side," Josephine continued. "Don't you see any difference between them?"

"Well, of course, Winona is an unusually handsome girl," I murmured. "Besides, she is younger."

"Younger!" groaned Josephine, evidently believing me hopeless. "Do you really, seriously think, Fred, that they are to be mentioned in the same breath as ladies?"

I rather think I looked foolish and twiddled my fingers.

"If," said Josephine, with an emphasis on the conjunction, and repeating it still more emphatically, "if it were necessary I would not say a word. If Winona were one of seven girls, I should be sorry, but I would not say a word. If it had been Josie, I should have been rather pleased—which shows, Fred, that I am not altogether hostile to the spirit of the age. But I am not prepared as yet to see my only really handsome daughter—and such a handsome one, Fred—fly in the face of convention and custom merely—merely to please Miss Jacket and the people who never have a chance to go anywhere."

All Josephine's combativeness and pride of opinion seemed to ooze suddenly away, and she buried her face on my shoulder, murmuring—

"Oh, yes, the whole system of society for girls is ridiculous and degenerating. I know it, I know it perfectly well. I don't approve of it, I never have approved of it. I wonder that so many come out of it as well as they do. And they are not content as in my day to be merely giddy; they go in now for smoking cigarettes and drinking liqueurs after dinner, and some of them paint their faces. Not all of them, of course, not one-tenth of them; Josie will never do anything of the kind. I ought, though, to be thankful, heartily thankful, if Winona prefers to stay away from all this and to develop worthy tastes of her own. She shall do what she pleases, Fred, only——"

My darling stopped short as though she had concluded not to complete her sentence. She gulped bravely and lifted her eyes to mine.

"Kiss me, dear," she whispered. "I am not really so worldly as you think."

"You are an angel, and will never be anything else to me," I responded, stroking her hair.

She lay still for a moment, happy but pensive. "She shall do whatever she pleases; only it is a very much easier matter for you to be virtuous and to say, 'Let her study medicine,' than for me."

"I have not said so, dearest."

"You have thought so, though. You do not need to speak to have me know when you are thinking things. No man can possibly conceive what it means to a mother to have a daughter a radiant beauty and peculiar."

"I dare say not," I murmured, humbly.

"Especially," she continued, reflectively, "when you consider that, though society is foolish, there is really nothing else at present to take its place to give a girl what nothing else is likely to give her—I do not say nothing else can give it to her, but nothing else is in the least likely to; and when you consider the vast number of wives and mothers who have been through it all when they were young, and are charming and—yes, Fred, sensible, intelligent women to-day. I don't pretend that I myself am half what I might have been, but I went through it all as a girl without becoming absolutely vapid and volatile. Didn't I, dear?"

"You certainly did, Josephine. If Winona turns out your equal I shall be more than satisfied."

"Thank you, dear, but you mustn't say it. I do wish her to have more mind. My mind was more or less neglected; but, on the other hand, Fred, I never had the opportunity to be peculiar, for there was no chance to be in those days. Now the disease is liable to break out in any family. All we can do, Fred, is to remember that we are growing old, and to trust that the world of to-day is wiser than we."

"Amen!" I murmured.

And yet the consciousness that Josephine passed through it all and is what she is, makes me feel a little doubtful still on the score of the new dispensation, in spite of the mushrooms with rich gray gravy.

VII

MY daughter Winona has become a Christian Scientist, and Josephine says I have only myself to blame in that I encouraged her to model herself upon Miss Jacket. This strikes me as a little harsh, seeing that Miss Jacket, M.D., is a regular practitioner in the allopathic line, whereas Winona declares that the science of medicine is all nonsense, for the excellent reason that there is no such thing as disease. When I used this argument as a defence, Josephine regarded me scornfully, and remarked that the pair were practically one in ideas, and that it was futile of me to split straws on such a point. Ye gods and little fishes! Is it, forsooth, splitting straws to maintain that there can be no sympathy of soul between a woman doctor who takes you at your word and administers castor-oil to cure your stomach-ache and one who elevates her nose and vows that you haven't one?

"You can't make fish of one and flesh of another," continued my wife, majestically. "The mischief was done when they walked arm-in-arm for weeks together while they were becoming intimate. It makes little difference, it seems to me, as to the precise nature of the development. If Winona hadn't embraced (as she calls it) Christian Science, she would in all probability have worn bloomers, in which case I should not have held Dr. Cora Jacket guiltless merely because that young woman continued to wear petticoats. Neither do I in the present emergency. Who was it introduced Winona to Mrs. Titus, I should like to know?"

"Was Miss Jacket responsible for that?" I inquired, respectfully, not venturing to contest further the soundness of my wife's logic in her present excited frame of mind.

"She was indeed, and it is very little consolation to me that she professes to be sorry for it now." Josephine tapped her foot with a worried air, which found voice presently in a laugh born of sheer desperation. "Isn't it perfectly ludicrous, Fred? Do you realize what the child wishes to do?"

"I understood you to state that she wishes to enter upon a crusade to show that all our aches and pains are hallucinations. There ought to be a fortune in that, my dear, compared with which the profits from David's electrical discovery will pale into insignificance."

"This is no laughing matter, Fred. She is intensely in earnest; her heart is set upon the plan, and there is no use in arguing with her. She simply looks calm and tells you that you don't know."

I scratched my head and pondered. My younger daughter's plan, as it had been unfolded to me, was this : She proposed to set up as a practitioner of Christian Science in partnership with another young woman of the same faith. They were to cure disease apparently by dint of assuring their patients that because there is no such thing as matter, nothing could be the matter with any one. Their instructress, Mrs. Titus, had demonstrated the truth of this theory by a varied line of cures, and they had been encouraged by her to go on with the good work. Had I any objection to the scheme?

"Perhaps I had better talk the matter over with her and try to bring her to her senses," I remarked.

"I wish you joy of the experience," said my wife, with a wry smile. "She is like a seraph in her serenity, and I might just as well have been talking to a stone wall for all the effect my words seemed to have. Of course you can prevent her; she understands that; but I should like to see you alter her opinion."

I concluded to try. Accordingly, I summoned Winona to the library that evening, and we were closeted with folded doors, as the phrase is, for an hour and a half. Being a father I was desirous naturally to be judicious and yet sympathetic; being a philosopher, I was willing to be enlightened if I was ignorant. My son David had demonstrated to me that a young germ of tuberculosis has all the engaging attractiveness of a six months' old baby ; perhaps it had been reserved for my daughter to prove to me that I had never had constitutional headaches. If so, what an amount of unnecessary misery I had undergone from sheer lack of knowledge !

Conventional conceptions are slow to relax their grip even when one's reason is prepared to discard them as out-worn. I am not giving utterance in this sententious fashion to distrust in allopathy ; I simply am thinking of the qualms which persisted in harrowing my soul as I gazed upon my very beautiful daughter, and tried to feel proud that she was endeavoring to do something useful. My associations with lovely women are so intimately associated with the ball-room floor and the purlieus of polite society, that, in spite of my secret sympathy with the progress of the sex, I could not completely school my mental machinery so as to exclude a lurking regret that such arrant good looks were to be wasted upon people who had nothing the matter with them, and who would, perhaps, be slow in recognizing the fact. I was even weak enough to remark :

"Winona, my dear, you look this evening handsome enough to eat."

As Christian Scientists are said to harbor the belief that, owing to the non-existence of matter, looks of any kind are a delusion and snare, for the reason that individuals do not really exist, but are merely so many reflections of the one eternal and immutable existence, just as the various reflections in a stream are often but the continuous duplication of some single incandescent jet, it was scarcely to be expected that my darling daughter would fall a victim to the lure which I held out to her. She had the goodness to smile a ghost of a smile, but it was evident that the speech interested her very little. Before settling down to the business in hand I could not help, however, saying to myself that, if I were a young man, I should fall down and worship before this particular shrine, Christian Science and delusion to the contrary notwithstanding. Then I said, with as much cheer as I could muster :

"And so you wish to practise medicine, Winona?"

"Not medicine, father. It is Christian Science."

"Excuse me. But are not Christian Scientists doctors?"

"We do not give medicine."

"But you cure sick people?"

Winona shook her head and smiled sweetly. "There are no sick people," she said, with quiet decision.

"Then why are there so many physicians?"

"If people had the requisite faith, there would be no more physicians."

"Only Christian Scientists."

My daughter looked at me no less sweetly because of my taunt, and responded:

"In time we shall all be able to heal ourselves. It is simply a question of strength and degree. Some of us have more power than others at present, but as the world grows the number of those sufficient unto themselves will increase."

"What makes you think so?"

"I know it, father."

"From Mrs. Titus?"

"Mrs. Titus knows it too ; but I know it not merely because she knows it, but because I can feel that it is so."

"But, my dear child, surely you do not mean to tell me that if I were to have typhoid fever, I shouldn't have it?"

"I know that you would think you had it."

"Well, supposing I died, wouldn't I be dead?"

Winona hesitated for an instant, but it was only in order to avoid committing herself to one heresy while seeking to avoid another. "You would be dead, though perhaps not as we now understand being dead. You would not have died of typhoid fever, but of the belief that you were suffering from typhoid fever induced by the hallucination of error."

"I see," I answered, though to tell the truth I did not, and it was very evident to me that Winona thought so too, for her serene smile revealed just a tinge of amusement. Even a real philosopher would be apt to feel nettled were he to suspect that he was making himself ridiculous in the eyes of his most beautiful daughter. I said a little sternly :

"I wish you would explain to me, in the first place, what you mean by saying that I might not be dead as we now understand being dead."

Winona folded her hands. "I said that, father, because we Christian Scientists are not yet certain as to what is the precise nature of death. There are some who deem death also an hallucination, and the apparent annihilation of matter consequent upon it merely a reflex confirmation of the truth that there is no matter, only spirit; and it may well be that as the world grows in faith, death will disappear in that we shall cease to think we see matter. Mrs. Titus holds this view, but I am not yet sufficiently free from error to be sure that I believe it."

"But you are sure you believe that I should not have typhoid fever?"

"Perfectly."

"But what if the doctors said I had?"

"They would be mistaken, father."

I stroked my chin in order to bridle my tongue. "How old are you, Winona?" I asked.

"Just eighteen, father."

"You have never studied medicine, I believe?"

"No."

"Nor had any special advantages or opportunities to investigate the nature of disease?"

"Only through Mrs. Titus."

"Precisely. And yet you are willing to call yourself wiser than the men who have devoted their lives to its study—the physicians of London, Paris, Berlin, and Vienna, to say nothing of those of New York and Boston."

A faint flush overspread Winona's face. "The doctors have been mistaken many times before, father. You remember Harvey and the circulation of the blood. The doctors laughed at him at first."

"But Harvey was a trained student of medicine; you are a school-girl."

"Mrs. Titus is not a school-girl."

"Has she ever studied medicine?"

"I think not. But as disease is simply human error, we consider the study of medicine a waste of time. Our faith teaches us that everything which doctors call illness is merely a clouding of truth in the soul by error."

"And how do you cure your patients who suffer from the error of typhoid fever?"

"By the restoration of truth and their faith in truth."

"By what active means? What do you do?"

"We think of them. We bring our minds to bear upon the error in their minds."

"Is that all?"

"It is sufficient, father. Mrs. Titus has effected wonderful cures by this means only."

"Does she cure all her patients?"

"When she does not cure them, it is because error has blinded them to the perception of truth. If all could perceive truth, there would be no more error; and, as it is, there are many who cannot perceive as yet even faintly."

"And this is all?"

"Yes, provided you understand."

"I understand the fundamental truth to be that matter does not exist."

"It does not."

"So that even our bodies are a sham."

"We believe that our bodies exist, but they do not really."

"Then why do you believe it?"

"I do not believe it, but I am not yet conscious that my body does not exist. I hope to be some day, yet very likely I shall never be. Mrs. Titus is conscious of the truth at times."

"Why do you say 'at times?'"

"Because she is still somewhat sensitive to the error of heat and cold. She considers this a weakness, and she is willing to admit that she is not wholly free from error. You see, Mrs. Titus is a perfectly reasonable woman, father. I am sure you would think so, if you could hear her talk. I heard her questioned the other day on that very point of susceptibility to cold. Some one asked —and asked in a scoffing spirit, father:

'Supposing you were to go out-doors, Mrs. Titus, with nothing on, when the thermometer was below zero, should you feel cold?' Her answer was: 'I fear I should, though I ought not to. It is possible that after a while I might be proof against the weakness, but in all probability I should never be able to overcome it. It is simply a question of time, though, when Christian Science is able to subdue this error.' Was that not unassumingly and beautifully put, father?"

"Quite unlike the brutal dogmatism of the regular practitioner, who would be apt to recommend a strait-jacket for the individual who should venture to brave the rigor of our New England climate without a stitch of clothing."

Although I spoke with a sober and sympathetic mien, my beautiful daughter plainly distrusted the sincerity of my words. Her great brown eyes regarded me mournfully, and it seemed to me there was pity in them —pity for her poor benighted parent. She said, sweetly and softly:

"You must not make sport of Christian Science, father. It has done a great deal of good already. Besides, Mrs. Titus did not do anything of the kind. There is nothing in the least sensational about her."

"And you wish to follow in her footsteps, my dear?

"I should like to try to."

"And what if I should forbid you to do anything of the sort?"

Winona's cheek flushed and her eyes dropped a little in the face of my appearance of sternness, but she answered with the same ineffable sweetness, as though she were seeking to impress upon me that persecution could not ruffle the temper of one of her faith. "I should have to give up the plan, of course. But," she murmured, "I should still be a Christian Scientist. I could not help being one, you know."

If you ask me why I did not remand her to afternoon teas and the mantua-makers, or advise her to allay her skipping spirit with some cold drops of philanthropy, I fear that I could not give a very satisfactory explanation. I am not, and I never shall be, a Christian Scientist, notwithstanding my beauty of a daughter declares that she can cure the proletariat of coughs, colics, and fevers simply by thinking about them. It was Josephine, not I, who remarked, after the matter was settled, and Winona had begun to keep office hours, that on the whole it was less dreadful than if she had become an actress or joined a settlement of the Toynbee Hall variety, for the reason that she still remained at home, and we had not wholly lost our hold upon her. Evidently Josephine regards her behavior as a passing phase which will sooner or later wear off and leave her more like other people, and she considers the actual practice of Christian Science rather less demoralizing, from a conventional point of view, than some other forms of revolt. I can see what she means. However honorable her intentions, a woman who has knocked about on the stage for half a dozen years is likely to have her perspective of life enlarged to such an extent that she can behold without winking many things which are carefully hidden from the general run of the sex, and the consequence is that she is apt to refuse to wear blinders for the rest of her existence. So, too, it can be safely predicated that continuous exalted fellowship with the dregs of the population on the part of women weaned from the lap of luxury, and a consequent sacrifice of almost every form of creature comfort, barring a tooth-brush, a small piano, a few books, and an etching or two, will be likely to create a sterner and sterner disrelish for the ice-cream and mushrooms vista of life at the end of which stands a husband with a newly furnished house and an ample income. My wife is ready to admit that purely from the point of view of common sense she would have preferred to have the child do almost anything peculiar rather than engage in her present mummery, because some people will consider her crazy; but, on the other hand, she maintains that the chances of losing her altogether are much less serious than if she had become a Toynbee Haller, for instance. "Mind you," said Josephine, "however much I might have fumed, I should really have been very, very proud if she had gone in for that.

I can imagine, if you once got used to the idea, feeling quite as happy over it as if one's son had become a clergyman, which of course," she added, meditatively, " is a peculiar kind of happiness not just like any other. But it would have meant separation forever, to all intents and purposes, for I am too old to change my interests now, however much I may disapprove of them in theory, and though I should very likely go in for something of the same kind in case I were to begin life over again. But I don't feel as though this Christian Science were more than a temporary craze ; and being just the ordinary every-day woman I am, I cannot help welcoming the possibility that Winona in course of time will come to her senses. It may be selfish of me, but I can't help it."

Now, I do not regard the matter from quite such a personal point of view as Josephine, though I agree with her that I should not have picked out Christian Science as the most desirable loop-hole of escape from the trammels of convention. To be sure, as Josephine says, it is her loss rather than mine, for a father is much less completely estranged from a daughter who is peculiar than is a mother, in that the bond of clothes and parties and all the hitherto traditional tastes of woman does not exist between a father and daughter. Hence it is probably much easier for me to look at the matter philosophically than it is for Josephine. Accordingly, though I laugh in my sleeve at the solemn pretensions of my dear deluded daughter, and am more or less uncomfortable in consequence of my consciousness that all the sensible people of my acquaintance are laughing at her also, I am inclined to watch her progress with a sympathy which includes the hope that she will work out of her present state of lunacy into a more practical field, rather than that she will relapse into the stereotyped woman whom we all know. When, however, Josephine asked me the other day to specify the field, I was obliged to admit that my ideas were a trifle hazy. My state of mind doubtless proceeds from a rooted conviction that the emancipation of woman has only just begun, and a certain sympathetic curiosity with her each and every effort to advance. To realize her progress, I have only to glance up at my ancestor with the mended eye and consider what a doll and a toy she was to him. Then I look at my wife, who was brought up on the old system, and say to myself that, unless indeed, man is to be utterly snuffed out and extinguished, there are certain feminine characteristics in the preservation of which he is deeply interested, even when, like myself, he is at heart an aider and abettor of emancipation. No more gingerbread education, no more treatment as dolls and nincompoops, no more discrimination between one sex and the other as to knowledge of this world's wickedness, no more curtailment of personal liberty on the score of that bugaboo, propriety—all these, if you like, ladies ; but we men, we fathers and philosophers, ask that you retain, for our sakes, beauty of face and form, beauty of raiment, low, modulated voices, and a graceful carriage, faith, hope, and charity, even though you continue to reveal these last-named as at present with sweet, illogical inconsequence. More than this, we cannot do without the tender devotion, the unselfish forethought, the aspiring faith, which, even though we seem to mock and to be blind, saves us from the world and from ourselves. If you are to become merely men in petticoats, what will become of us ? We shall go down, down, down, like the leaden plummet cast into the depths of the sea. We shall be snuffed out and extinguished in sober truth. Hence, certain that the work of emancipation is to continue, my philosophical glance follows fondly and almost proudly the course of my second daughter, who is making a fool of herself at the moment by practising Christian Science, because she has beauty and grace and a knowledge of the value of colors, purity and tenderness and aspiring faith, as her mother had before her, while at the same time she has forsaken the beaten path of convention and turned her brow to the morning. All of which, Josephine informs me, is charming reasoning, provided Winona does not fall in love with somebody. I do not understand the precise logic of this criticism ; but, on the other hand, Josephine is very apt to know what she is talking about.

VIII

I CAME home one afternoon with a puckered brow.

"Has the Supreme Court decided another case against you?" asked Josephine, with solicitude.

I shook my head, and answered wearily: "Worse than that."

My wife regarded me in anxious silence, while manifestly she was cudgelling her brains to divine what could have happened. As she told me afterward, she imagined, from my doleful air, that I must at least have a seed in my little sac.

"They have asked me to run for Congress in this district," I finally vouchsafed to state.

Josephine dropped her fancy-work and sat upright with an air of satisfaction which was wholly out of keeping with my own dejected mien.

"Really, Fred! Who has asked you? The Governor?"

"The Governor does not usually go round on his bended knees asking candidates to run for Congress," I answered, with mild sarcasm.

"Well, the Mayor then?"

I have labored for years to make plain to Josephine the ramifications of our National, State, and Municipal Government; but just as I am beginning to think that she understands the matter tolerably well, she is sure to break out in some such hopeless fashion as this, which shows that her conceptions are still crookeder than a ram's horn. And the strangest part is that she can tell you all about the English Parliament and Home Rule, and whether any given statesman is a Liberal or a Liberal Unionist, and about M. Clemenceau and the relative strength of the Bonapartists and Orleans factions. But when it comes to distinguishing clearly between an Alderman and a State Senator, or a

Member of Congress and a Member of the Legislature, she is apt to get exasperatingly muddled. I asked her once, in my most impressive manner, why it was that she did not take a more vital interest in the politics of her native country, and after reflecting a moment, she told me that she thought it must be because they were so stupid. On the other hand, with apparent inconsistency, she has many times expressed the hope that I would some day be conspicuously connected with them. I have been conscious for some time that it would suit her admirably to have me round off my professional career as Speaker of the National House of Representatives or Minister to the Court of St. James.

"Josephine," I said, in a tone of despair, "have I not explained to you time and time again that Members of Congress are the Representatives from the several States who are sent to Washington? How could the Governor, who is a State officer, or the Mayor, who is a municipal officer, have anything to do with the nomination of a Member of the

National House of Representatives? Only think, dear, what you are saying."

Probably Josephine would have evinced more contrition in tribute to this harangue had not her ears been fascinated by my reference to the Capital of our country.

"It *was* stupid of me, Fred. Do you mean to tell me, dear, they are going to send you to Washington? That would be perfectly delightful."

"I merely have been asked to accept the nomination for Congress in the Fourth District," I answered, dryly.

"And what did you tell them?"

"I said I would think it over."

"You must accept. Of course you will accept? It would be splendid, Fred. I would a great deal rather have you in Congress than go on our trip to Japan. I have often thought I should like to pass a winter in Washington."

By dint of economy and some shrewd investments I had managed to save up a vacation fund of more than normal size, by means of which Josephine and I were proposing to enjoy a jaunt to Japan. We had been looking forward to this excursion, which I felt that we had fairly earned by strict devotion to home and business ties for a long period of years.

"The district is hopelessly Republican, in the first place, my dear, and I, as you know, am a Democrat."

Josephine looked grave for a moment. "But a great many Republicans would vote for you, Fred. Oh, I am sure they would!" she added, eagerly, impressed by the plausibility of the idea. "Harry Bolles is a Republican, and I am certain he would vote for you; so would Dr. Meredith and Sam Bangs."

"They are three out of several thousand voters in the district, Josephine. You argue like the committee which waited upon me."

"They said a great many Republicans would vote for you, didn't they? And they thought you would be elected?"

"They were kind enough to state that I had a good fighting chance; which means, my dear, that I haven't the ghost of a show."

Josephine regarded me a moment distrustfully. "It doesn't seem to me there is any use in being too modest about such a matter as this, Fred. Somebody has to be elected, and it might as well be you as anybody. I have always hoped you would go into politics, you know. If they hadn't wanted you they wouldn't have asked you."

"The only certain thing about it is, that, if they had supposed I could possibly be elected, they wouldn't have offered me the nomination."

"What do you mean, Fred? I call that mock modesty, darling."

I did not consider that I was called upon to unfold more particularly to my wife the cynical estimate of the case which I entertained in my secret soul, especially in view of the fact that the committee which had waited upon me comprised not merely politicians, but some of our best citizens. Although a man who is invited to run for Congress in a district hopelessly hostile is likely to cherish secret suspicions as to the sincerity of those who offer him the nomination, the bait of self-sacrifice for the public good has lured many a cleverer man than I to his destruction. Besides, a fighting chance invariably seems more prodigious to the one who is said to have it, than to anyone else. There were certainly weak joints in the armor (an analogy supplied me by the committee) of my opponent, who was a dyed-in-the-wool politician, and indisputably I had a great many friends. Could I afford to disregard the piteous, eloquent argument of the spokesman, Honorable David Flint, that the sacred cause of Reform demanded me as its champion, and that victory was possible only under my banner? I had promised to think it over, which was a coy way of stating that I would accept. Having made up my mind to run, I was obliged to tell Josephine that this would mean good-by for many a long and weary month to our jaunt.

"If you're elected, Fred, I shall be only too glad to postpone it. And if by any chance you don't get in, we'll forget all about it in dear Japan."

"You do not quite understand the situation, pet. We stay at home in any case, election or no election. The expenses will eat up my savings for a rainy day in Japan. I shall have to contribute handsomely to everybody and everything. It's an outrage, but one of the painful results of having greatness thrust upon one."

Thereupon Josephine flung her arms around my neck and informed me that I was not only a dear, noble hero, but that Japan or no Japan, she would not begrudge one copper of any sum I might be obliged to spend in order to defeat that odious wretch, Mr. Daniel Spinney. A few days later, after my letter of acceptance was published, she said that she did not see how anyone who had the least respect for the sacred right of suffrage could hesitate between us.

"Spinney is not such a bad fellow at bottom," I replied, albeit touched by the warm partisanship of my wife.

" Didn't I read in the newspaper this morning that he is a notorious spoilsman ? "

"Very likely, dear. Spinney has always called Civil Service Reform a humbug."

" And he is all wrong on the tariff."

"We think so."

"Well, then, how can you say that he isn't a bad fellow at bottom?"

"I mean, Josephine, that apart from politics he is a very decent sort of person. I couldn't help thinking while I was chatting with him yesterday that there was something quite attractive about him. He isn't exactly the kind of man I should hold up as a model to my sons, but, as I said before, he is by no means a bad fellow."

Josephine had been looking at me aghast ever since the opening sentence of this speech. "You don't mean to tell me, Fred, that you stopped and chatted with that wretch?"

"Indeed I do. We happened to meet, and so we hobnobbed for five minutes on the street corner and drew each other out in the friendliest sort of fashion as to our mutual prospects. He says he has a walk-over, and I told him that he isn't in it."

"I'm glad you showed a little spirit, anyhow."

"What would you have had me do? Make a fell assault upon his hair and eyeballs?

As it was, I perpetrated a deliberate falsehood in the good cause. He knows that I know I am beaten from the start."

"Nonsense," said Josephine. "You provoke me, Fred, when you talk in that fashion. What was the use of accepting if you didn't intend to win if you could?"

"So I do intend, but I can't."

"You can't certainly if you hobnob with the rival candidate and call him a good fellow."

"You ought to have been a politician, Josephine."

"No, I'm only crazy to have you win, Fred, and I'm convinced you can win if you only think so yourself and pitch in as if you thought so. I dare say Mr. Spinney may be well enough apart from politics, but it is politics we are interested in at present, and it seems to me it is your duty to hate him— until the election is over, anyway. If you defeat him, you may ask him to dinner, if you like."

Her eyes sparkled like diamonds, and there was a dangerous look in them which would have boded ill for Mr. Spinney or any other Republican had he happened to thrust his head inside our doors just then. As for me, I felt a little sheepish at my lack of courage, I must confess, and I cried with genuine ardor: "Hurrah for Reform! You're right, my dear," I added, "I must pitch in. I haven't been quite so pusillanimous, however, as it would seem, for I have got Nick Long to superintend my campaign."

You may remember that Nicholas Long, or Nick Long, as we always speak of him, has never stood high in Josephine's good graces on account of his unorthodox habits regarding church-going. He has an unpleasant way of encountering us on our way to the sanctuary in the toggery of a man who is going to take a day off in the country. He has, however, a cool, analytical mind, and his name has been associated for some years with reform politics. In obtaining his services as a manager I felt that I had done well and wisely. Josephine looked a little sober, as though she was not altogether gratified at my selection, but realizing, very likely on second thought, that the children's habits were formed, she contented herself by remarking :

"I shall keep my eye upon him and make sure that he doesn't get you into any mischief."

"You seem to forget," I said, "that he is a leading reformer."

Josephine smiled incredulously. "Fred," she continued presently, with a pensive air, "I wish it were the custom here, as it is in England, for a candidate's wife to go about and buttonhole people and beg votes and kiss babies for him, and all that sort of thing. I'm not so young as I was, I know, but I dare say I should appear quite as well as Mrs. Daniel Spinney, whoever she may be. I really think I could make a fairly respectable speech just on the strength of my conjugal devotion and righteous indignation against that villain of a man. 'Ahem : Fellow Democrats, I beseech you in the name of common sense and decency, in the name of the Goddess of Liberty, and of good government and order, and as you love your cradles and your firesides, not to vote for that dyed-in-the-wool Republican and spoilsman, Daniel Spinney, but to vote early and often for that talented, noble, self-sacrificing, upright citizen and Democrat, Frederick ———.'"

"*E pluribus unum!* Let her go, Gallagher! Erin go bragh! rah! rah! rah! Harvard!" I cried, as I seized the lovely orator in my arms and hugged her to my breast, thereby, to adopt her own words, squeezing out of her the little breath which she had left. "Bravo, Josephine! If you were to take the stump it would be I and not Mr. Spinney who would have a walk-over."

"At any rate, Fred," she continued, after she had regained her breath and recomposed her ruffled hair, "I can put in a word to help you here and there among our friends. It was on the tip of my tongue yesterday to call Rev. Bradley Mason's attention to the fact that you were a candidate, in the hope that he might make just a slight allusion to it from the pulpit. Not directly by name, of course; he couldn't do that very well; but he might speak of the importance of aiding those who were battling for the noble cause of pure government, so that people could guess what he meant. I didn't do it," she added, a little ruefully, "because I was afraid you might possibly not like it, and there was plenty of time in which to give him the hint."

"Thank goodness you didn't say a word on the subject," I answered. "It wouldn't have done at all."

For the next six weeks our house was a veritable bureau of political activity. Although Josephine lived up to her threat of keeping an eye on Nicholas Long, she admitted before many days had passed that he was what my boys call a thorough-going hustler, and that he was determined to leave no portion of my Congressional acreage unsown with Democratic seed. This farming metaphor was borrowed from Nick, who had many others at his command suited to the various classes of constituents he wished to reach. His brain fairly buzzed with fertile expedients devised to catch this and that portion of the popular vote. He was a great believer in documents. As he expressed it, the territory must be plastered with statistics and other printed matter, which were much more serviceable nowadays than in the past. He said that formerly the average voter flung everything into the waste-basket and went to the polls simply on the strength of party prejudice fortified by the glamour of a torchlight procession, but that now he read and thought, and refused to support the party candidate merely because he was the party candidate. He deluged the community with copies of my letter of acceptance, and three days later overwhelmed the postal service with a batch of circulars embodying a short, pithy description of my personal virtues and talents, interwoven with sound doctrine. Although he confided to me that torchlight organizations were moribund factors in political warfare, he advised me to supply uniforms and torches, and a promise of abundant cigars, ice-cream, and ginger-beer for the cementation of a band of youthful warriors eager to call themselves the "Fourth District Reform Cadets." "There is not more than one voter in twenty among them," said Nick, "but it will please their fathers, and do no harm in any event, especially as your wife and I have devised a costume for them that will drive the Spinney Guards under cover with jealousy."

The costume in question was a pattern of garish ingenuity : white bearskin caps with red, white, and blue pompons ; bright blue blouses dashed with white, and white leather belts, and red zouave knickerbockers. Their torches were encased in fantastic glass lanterns alternately red, white, and blue. On the occasion of their first parade, when they drew up before the house to receive their transparency, adorned on one side with a villainous portrait of myself superscribed by the motto, "Our Fathers Fought For Freedom, We Are Fighting For The Right," and on the other a cut depicting the rival candidate up to his armpits in the bog of Civil Service Reform, described as "Spinney's Walk-Over" (a happy blending, as Nick called it, of serious principle and humorous suggestion), I appeared on the door-steps and delivered a few halting sentences of gratitude and augury for success, which were received with loud plaudits and the rattle of the drum corps. Thereupon I invited the battalion to enter and partake of a little simple hospitality, which they hastened to do to the number of two hundred, including a dozen ward heelers in citizens' raiment, and three or four nondescripts whom nobody knew, but whom Nick said it would be impolitic to offend by exclusion. A hearty supper was ready for them in the dining-room, presided over by Josephine and her daughters, whose presence seemed at first to abash my warriors of the torch. But only for a few moments. Realizing presently that these Goddesses had apparently but one aim in life, to wit, to help them to salad, oysters, and ice-cream, diffidence disappeared like fog before the morning sun, and with it the viands down the throats of my red, white, and blue supporters. In the liquid line Josephine gave a choice of hot coffee and chocolate, thereby joining issue for the first time with my manager on the subject of methods. Nick was in favor of champagne, on the score that the Spinney Guards had been regaled with beer and sherry, but my darling declared that even if it were the turning-point of the election, she would not consent to win votes by playing Hebe to beardless youths. A political aspirant who is forced to decide between his manager and his wife has need of all the philosophy at his command.

To atone for this obduracy, Josephine had a pleasant little surprise ready in the shape of a basket of silken badges emblematic chiefly of myself, and more remotely of the Presidential candidate and our party principles. She and her daughters, despite my blushes, fastened these one by one to the blue blouses of the members of the Fourth District Reform Cadets after everything to eat and drink in the house had vanished. Not only then, but henceforth until the end of the campaign, it was embarrassing to me to note how subordinate a position every other candidate held in Josephine's regard. One would have supposed that I was the party nominee for the chief magistracy of the nation, instead of the leader of a forlorn contest for a congressional seat in a hopelessly Republican district. On the occasion of the torchlight parade two miles long, whereby the enemy sought to carry the city by storm, and which passed close to our front door, our house was as dark as Erebus. Josephine insisted even that the lights in the front hall and in the basement should be extinguished, and she drew the drawing-room curtains over the window-shades so that we need not seem to furnish our foes with one pale ray of comfort. Induced by curiosity to peep out at the passing show, she limited her strictures to scornful but tranquil denunciation of the campaign rhetoric blazoned on the transparencies, until the Spinney Guards arrived, headed by a magnificent mulatto bearing a delineation of the Reform Candidate submerged in a huge soup-tureen with an appropriate tag beneath. For an instant she stared, then she gasped as though some one had struck her, and she fiercely started to raise the window.

"What are you trying to do, Josephine?"

"Let me go, Fred. I will, I will. How dare they?"

"Pooh, dear! All is fair in politics. It's no worse than the Swamp of Civil Service Reform," I said, as I tore away her vindictive grasp from the window which she had succeeded in opening a foot or two, and shut it hastily.

"How dare they? You had no right to prevent me from hissing, Fred. I should like to fling something at them too. It's an outrage making you look like that, and—and in the soup, too."

Not all the enthusiasm generated by our rival procession, which took place forty-eight hours later, nor indeed the long flattering list of my supporters published by Nick Long in the newspaper for two days prior to election day, sufficed entirely to obliterate from Josephine's soul the bitterness of this insult. As she expressed it, was it not cruel to flaunt such a thing in the faces of children who had been used to think of their father as the most dignified of men, one with whose personality no one would dare to tamper or trifle? It nerved her, however, to more desperate efforts in my behalf. She ventured even on holding up our beloved pastor, the Rev. Bradley Mason, in the street, and capturing his signature to the list of leading citizens who supported me. This ought, she declared, to outweigh sixty soup-tureens.

Before the votes were counted I knew well enough that I had been defeated, but for Josephine's dear sake I allowed her to prepare a victor's banquet, on the assumption that my friends would be pouring in upon me with congratulations. It was she who drove me from my evening paper, to which I was settling down like a philosopher after dinner, to go to my headquarters and ascertain the result. She was sure I was elected. If not (and here her voice melted) the people were not fit to have such a pearl offered to them. I went, and it was half-past ten when I returned. She heard my step, and rushed down to meet me at the front door. I was calm and smiling.

"Defeated by one hundred and fourteen votes, dear. A close fight, wasn't it?"

"Ah, Fred, defeated! You poor, poor boy."

"I can stand it if you can, Josephine," I answered, as with my arm wound around her waist I led her into the dining-room, where the stalled ox and truffled turkey and a glittering array of glass confronted us.

"It was that horrid soup-tureen did it, I am convinced," she murmured, sitting down beside me on the sofa.

"Nonsense, dear. Everyone says I got a wonderful vote against such odds. They are talking about it down town as though I had won a victory. Nick is called a great manager."

"But that Spinney is elected all the same," she said, dejectedly.

"Yes, he is, Josephine. We can't escape from that. I tell you what, I'm going to have a glass of champagne," I said, entering the china closet and taking possession of one of the bottles which had been packed in ice for the refreshment of my friends. I filled a glass for each of us and drained mine to the philosophical toast, "Here's to peace and a quiet life, my dear."

"It would have been very nice to go to Washington," said Josephine, between her sips. "It might have been a stepping-stone to higher things. You know you would be pleased to be sent abroad as a foreign minister. It would have just suited you, Fred."

"It may be that the President, when he hears of the gallant fight I made, will reward me with something in that line," I answered, with a twinkle in my eye. "By the way, what egotists we are! I did not tell you, and you did not inquire, who had been elected President. We have won a glorious victory."

"I'm very glad, I'm sure," said Josephine, in a tone which was scandalously absent-minded considering the importance of the information. After a moment she remarked, coyly: "I should really think, Fred, there might be a chance of his giving you something when he hears."

"Not the slightest, you dear woman. I was only teasing you. I am a very humble figure in the politics of the country, I assure you, and even if the President is aware of my existence when he enters office, it will never occur to him to pick me out for preferment. Besides, I don't wish anything. I am perfectly content to sink back into the obscurity from which I was lured by the call of duty.

It would have tickled my pride a little to defeat Spinney, but I am inclined to think I should have found it rather a bore to be only one Congressman among so many."

"Just think of it, one hundred and fifteen more votes would have given you the election. It seems hard to have missed it by so little. You mustn't think me a goose about you, Fred," she added, after a thoughtful pause. I don't usually praise you to your face and make an undue fuss about you, do I, dear? I think I am disposed to be critical of you rather than otherwise. But you are so much superior to the men they generally put up, that I'm unable to reconcile myself to the idea that you're not to be anything distinguished after all. Of course I didn't really expect that you were going to be very great; and yet in politics one cannot always tell. Men no more remarkable than you have been elected President; though I'm not at all sure that I should have cared to have you in the White House."

"Yet you will not cease to love me now that I am doomed to be only a poor private citizen for the rest of my days?" I asked, fondly, as my arm stole around her waist, which, though no longer wisp-like as of yore, is shapely still. "Poor, too, in every sense," I added, unpleasantly reminded by the pressure of the check-book in my coat-pocket of my sadly diminished bank account.

"I am afraid I should continue to love you, Fred, even if you were bad—a Daniel Spinney or a Nicholas Long, for example," she answered, imprinting a kiss upon my cheek. "But you are an angel, dear."

It was worth being defeated for Congress in order to learn how much my wife appreciated me, and also to learn to appreciate her more thoroughly, philosophical deductions which I whispered in her ear with appropriate circumlocution. "But, Josephine," I added, "why do you include Spinney and Nick Long in the same category of wickedness?"

"Because they are both wicked."

"But Nick is a reformer, my dear."

"Hasn't he nearly ruined you?"

"I had to hand over a great deal of money to him, certainly," I answered, ruefully.

"What did he spend it for?"

"I didn't ask him for the details, but he always said he needed it for printing, dear. You know there was a great deal of printing done," I hastened to add, feeling a little nervous under the stress of cross-examination. "Then there were the uniforms and the torches and the supper for the cadets."

"I know what they cost exactly. Fred, what do you suppose he could have used all that money for?"

"Printing, I have told you, Josephine. There are all sorts of expenses in a campaign of this sort, the details of which one has to leave to one's manager. I have implicit confidence in Nick's good judgment," I continued, a trifle austerely. To tell the truth, I had been wondering myself where all the money had gone to. Josephine was thoughtful for several minutes, then she said: "Do you know, Fred, I have a feeling that if you had managed your own campaign without the aid of a reformer you would have got just as many votes—and—and we should have had money enough left to go to Japan."

If a woman has a prejudice against a man he might be spotless as the Archangel Gabriel, and she would be able to pick a flaw in him.

IX

SIX months ago an astonishing piece of news was revealed to me. Astonishing at least to me, though Josephine says that I need not have been astonished had I kept my eyes open, inasmuch as the affair was going on under my very nose, and everybody in town except myself knew how it was likely to end. I refer to my daughter Josie's engagement.

Yesterday I gave her away—a euphemistic way of stating that she was torn from my arms—to a young man of whom I know next to nothing, though I hear on all sides that he is a very nice fellow, which might mean that he is utterly without principle and an easy-going, idle, selfish hound. In appearance he does not seem to me to differ from nine-tenths of the young men who in the course of the last five years have said, "How d'y do?" or "Good-by" to me (rarely more or less) when they have run across me in my own drawing-room. My wife declares that he has a spiritual face, and that he reminds her of me at the same age, which I regard as an ingenious attempt to prepossess me in his favor. She has informed me also that Josie is over head and ears in love with him and he with Josie, a predicament on his part which I am not surprised at; and I suppose that I am bound to admit that my daughter is justified in her infatuation for him, if he resembles me at thirty.

Plainly, I have become an old cynic by reason of the loss of my dear Josie. I realize that I have been like a bear with a sore head ever since the ceremony. As for Josephine, she has been mooning about the house all day in a state of chronic tearfulness. The responsibility of the bride's appearance and the wedding collation kept her nerved until everything was over. Last evening she collapsed and fell asleep in my arms, sobbing like a child.

His name is James Perkins. I have been doing my best for several months to call him "Jim," as everybody else does, instead of "James," or "Perkins," and yesterday I succeeded twice in doing so. I had had three glasses of champagne. He is an architect, and I understand from Josie that he has already made his mark in the erection of a church, two school-houses, and a town-hall in the suburbs, which I have promised her to go and see. It seems that a week before he had the impertinence to offer himself to her he received word that his plans for a vast railroad station in one of the large Western cities had been accepted. But for this untoward circumstance, my dear Josie would still be the light of my house, and I should not be gnawing at my mustache in the throes of misanthropy.

Jim is slight and not very tall, and he does not look especially strong. They tell me that he has worked very hard, and that he has won his way purely by his own energy and talent. He does not smoke, which rather prejudiced me against him, in spite of the fact that I believe we should all be the healthier if we did not use tobacco. This, as Josephine would say, only shows what an inconsistent creature I am. And I a philosopher, too! But I said at the outset that I was not a real philosopher. Josie met James—I beg his pardon, Jim—at her coming-out party, and it seems that he fell in love with her at first sight. If, now, somebody had fallen in love at first sight with my sister-in-law, Julia, how much more satisfactory it would have been all round. But that is the way of the world; Julia was overlooked and my girl taken, to my miserable discomfiture. Jim was one of the youths without fathers and mothers whom you see at every large entertainment. That is to say, my wife had never heard of his father and mother at the time she invited him, though they prove to have been very respectable people. Indeed, we were all of us struck by the dignified appearance which his family as a whole presented at the wedding. Alas! I realize already that when I have got used to the idea that anybody is to have her, I shall be thoroughly happy in the thought that I have given her away to such a decent fellow, a man with self-respect and principles, a man of industry and capacity, and one, too, who is ready to drink his glass of champagne like the rest of the world—although he does not smoke. I have let my grudge have free scope, and all I have been able to rake up against him is that he shakes his head when I offer him a pipe or a cigar. In my secret soul I am egregiously proud of him already, and but for my wounded sensibilities I could dance with joy over the reflection that he is likely to make her perfectly happy. And yet all this talk of marrying and giving in marriage has broken my spirit.

"Since it had to be someone," I said by way of consolation to Josephine when we awoke this morning, "it's extremely fortunate that she did not fall in love with a dashing soldier, who would carry her off to a barracks on the frontier of a Sioux reservation, or a swashing sailor, who would leave her at home while he went on long cruises, or a splendid-looking creature, with a sonorous voice, who would drink himself into his grave or else make her miserable by devoting himself to another woman. Some of the nicest fellows I ever knew have made their wives thoroughly wretched. When you think that there really isn't anything very wonderful to look at about—er—Jim, that is, anything to appeal especially to the romantic side of a girl, I think it's very greatly to Josie's credit that she should have chosen him. Many girls might have overlooked his solid attractions and gone in for a Jim dandy of a chap who wasn't worth his salt."

My wife looked a little blank over this philosophic statement, then she glanced up at me with a roguish smile and said: "You seem to forget, dear, that I accepted you."

"True enough," I answered, merrily. "I dare say I wasn't a trifle less commonplace-looking than son-in-law. Besides we both have spiritual faces."

"You should give me and Josie credit for being able to see below the surface," said my darling, fondly. "A soldier or a sailor, or a splendid-looking creature such as you describe, is delightful at a party ; but gold buttons, or even a very handsome mustache, don't go far nowadays toward blinding a sensible girl to the fact that she will have to pass all her days with the man she chooses. You know, dear, that you and I have never believed that marriage is a lottery. We were sure of each other beforehand. So are Josie and Jim."

"Thank God that it is so ; and may he, darling, grant them such happiness as he has given us."

"Amen ! And, Fred, he—James" (Josephine prefers to call him James ; she thinks Jim undignified) "is not really homely. He isn't an Adonis, of course, and doesn't impress one especially at first glance, but anyone who looks at him twice can see that he is very intelligent, and that he has the appearance of a gentleman."

"Right you are, my dear. Perhaps I was unconsciously comparing him with the young man whom I met strolling with your other daughter not many days ago."

"With Winona? When?" she asked with a start.

"About dusk."

"No, no, on what day?"

"Let me see. It must have been a week ago yesterday."

"Who was he? Why didn't you tell me before?"

"He was tall, handsome, and impressive-looking," I replied, with quiet deliberation.

"What *do* you mean, Fred? How slow you are. Do go on."

"As to telling you before, I thought it best to wait until you had one of your girls off your mind. As to being slow, I have told you all there is to tell already. I met Winona about dusk a week ago yesterday in the company of a tall, handsome, impressive-looking young man whom I had never seen in my life. I don't know where they were going or where they came from or what it meant. I hope to see him again so as to say to him, 'Young man, beware ; I have lost one daughter, and I am in no mood to be trifled with.' I dare say," I continued, nonchalantly, "that if you were to keep your eyes open you would be able to see what is evidently going on under your very nose, my dear."

Josephine did not heed this taunt; she was thinking hard.

"I wonder who it could have been," she murmured, presently. "I have noticed lately that Winona has acted as though she had something on her mind; but I had assumed it might be because her patients were falling off, owing to the death of that woman with consumption who could not be persuaded that she had nothing the matter with her. It would be a great relief to my mind to see the dear girl happily married. What did he look like, Fred? Are you certain you have never seen him before? Just think: you're sure it wasn't Mr. Dyer or Mr. Benson? One might call either of them tall, handsome, and impressive-looking."

"I have told you everything I know, Josephine," I retorted, fiercely. "I don't know the man from Adam. I should think," I added, with a sepulchral outburst, "that after what happened yesterday, Josephine, you wouldn't be in so much haste to marry the only girl we have left."

"Excuse me, Fred," she said, gently. "It *was* cruel of me to suggest such a thing so soon. And yet I suppose we must be prepared for something of the kind sooner or later. You know you have constantly expressed the hope that neither of them would hang fire like dear Julia."

"Oh, I know it. I'm a selfish brute, Josephine," I answered, beginning to hone my razor with the desperate air of one who would fain cut his own throat as the simplest solution of the problem of living.

And only six months ago the horizon of my domestic happiness looked so clear and comforting. Not even a cloud of the traditional smallness of a man's hand marred its serenity. Little Fred was pegging away at Leggatt & Paine's with commendable steadiness all day, and, though he was apt to dance all night by way of making up for it, I was comforted in my solicitude regarding his health by the recollection that I used to do the same when I was his age, my spiritual countenance to the contrary notwithstanding. Besides, Leggatt has always a good word to say for him, and evidently still keeps an eye on him, notwithstanding that Fred has ceased to kick foot-ball and limps no longer. To be sure, I have been beguiled once or twice by the dear boy's assurance that I would make my fortune, if I would follow his advice, into buying investment securities the market price of which at present is far less than I paid for them. However, the financial misinformation imparted by one's own flesh and blood is more easily forgiven than that which emanates from one's regular broker. Besides, there is the chance that the stocks will come up again some day or other. Fred says they are sure to. Everything considered he was, and indeed he still is, doing remarkably well, and he is such an honest-looking, manly fellow that Josephine says she wonders all the girls do not fall in love with him. His present safety seems to lie in the fact that he is in love with all the girls and not with any particular one, a condition of affairs which I trust will last until he is properly able to support a wife. I remember that before I fell in love with Josephine—well, no matter. I have almost forgotten their names and should have to ask my darling to tell me who they were, and all about it. I have never really loved anybody but her, God bless her.

Then there was David—again I must admit there still *is* David—whose rapid success in his adopted profession and whose general steadiness of character have been a source of perpetual gladness to us. He still causes his mother some concern by his utter disinclination for the society of young women, but I know of no other fault with which to reproach him. His bacillic pets no longer have a domicile under the paternal roof. He has a laboratory of his own downtown where, doubtless, they thrive and multiply. But his special interest at present is electricity. This has already brought him reputation and money by virtue of an appliance in the storage battery line, the details of which I do not precisely understand. Although Little Fred shook his head gravely at the mention of the word "patent," I was imprudent enough to follow my scientific son's lead to the tune of several thousand dollars, the happy consequence of which seemed to be that Josephine and I would be able to have our jaunt to Japan whenever the spirit moved us. That was before I counted the cost of marrying a daughter.

Thirdly, there was that daughter, a dear, sweet girl, who seemed to me perfectly content in her enjoyment of the social pleasures in which she was so well adapted to shine. I regarded her as still a mere child, and though youths came and went, never for one moment did I suspect that she was meditating the blow which she has since inflicted upon me, until Josephine told me one evening, with a mysterious, agitated air, that Mr. James Perkins wished to see me in the library. He saw me, and all the consolation I derived from our interview was the impression that he considered that he was acting generously in asking my consent to the match, and that custom would have justified him in letting me hear the news of my daughter's engagement elsewhere and in seeing me further, as the phrase is, before he saw me at all. Remembering as

I did that I regarded the views of Josephine's father concerning our little matter twenty-five years ago as a matter of mere detail, only think how far I fell short of the temper of a real philosopher in allowing myself to become violently angry, and to pace the library until one o'clock in the morning after my would-be son-in-law had left it! An especially futile proceeding, as Josephine subsequently remarked, inasmuch as, by my own admission, I had behaved like a veritable lamb in his presence and had told him blandly that if he and my daughter were agreed upon the subject I had not a word to say against it.

This was the first break in our peaceful, happy domestic circle. Do you know what the period of an idolized daughter's engagement seems to the disdained and discarded husband and father? He is too shy and dignified to peep at the billing and cooing through the crack of the drawing-room door like the younger members of the family; consequently, the six months which intervene between the making of the match and its consummation, impress him as a Sahara of tedious confabulation between the pair of turtle doves as to whether they have too many salt-cellars for their marital needs, and whether the exchange of a third set of oyster-forks without the knowledge of the donor would be a violation of the highest code of ethics. Presents, presents, nothing but presents, of every kind and degree, from the solid silver tea-set of exquisitely fluted pattern to the excruciatingly ugly bit of *bric-à-brac* which has captivated the undiscerning eye of some dear friend. After every ring at the door-bell appears the maid with a fresh parcel wrapped in snow-white paper fastened with a dainty ribbon, and on each occasion my dear Josie's eyes sparkle more excitedly as she clutches it and frees it from its caparisons. And ever and anon I am struck by the fact that she is growing thin and pale. I mention it to Josephine, but she tells me that girls always get peaked before their weddings, and that she herself was thin as a rail at the time she married me. I get no sympathy anywhere. My sole connection with the matter is that I am to give the bride away.

I did so yesterday in the presence of our entire social acquaintance and their dressmakers, most of whom I subsequently entertained at a mid-day collation, where I shook hands with a vast array of young people whom I did not know, and tried to keep up my spirits by asking my old friends to take wine with me. It was after the third glass that the spirit moved me to address my new son-in-law as "Jim." An hour later I saw the young rascal carry off my Josie in a carriage with an air as though he owned her, and I could have strangled him. At the same moment I was unpleasantly conscious that a quantity of rice hurled by an enthusiastic miss of nineteen was going down my back. I made a mad rush forward like a bull; I don't know exactly what I had in mind to do, but I was bunted aside by a youth who, I am sure, could never have had a father and mother. He held an old shoe in his hand, which he proceeded to cast with such unerring aim that it landed on the top of the bridal coach, to the infinite delight of everybody except myself. I could see no especial humor in it, but

The Opinions of a Philosopher

Josephine tells me that we underwent precisely the same experience at our own wedding and thought it amusing. I perceive that it makes considerable difference in this world whose ox is gored, or, to put it more accurately, whether one is carrying off some other man's daughter or is being robbed of his own.

And now to crown all, I am haunted by the vision of Winona and that tall, handsome, impressive-looking young man in whose company I met her the other day about dusk. In saying to Josephine that I had told her all, I did not speak the truth in a certain sense. I did tell her all I knew, but I did not confide to her all that I suspected. I did not reveal to her that at the moment my eye fell upon them my only remaining daughter was gazing up into the face of her male companion with that peculiar look of absorbed attention which has so often wrought the ruin of Platonic friendship. It entered like iron into my parental soul, already quivering with its recent wound, and I murmured to myself, "Oh, my prophetic soul, my second son-in-law!"

Winona too! Two years have passed since I granted her permission to practise Christian Science, and from that time to this she has gone regularly every day to her office to minister to the patients who have applied to her for treatment. I am unable to state whether these have been many or few; to be frank, I have been amazed that she has had any at all. But I am sure that she has had some, and that she claims to have cured several sufferers from chronic disorders whom the regular practitioners had declared incurable. Or, more accurately, I should say that she has demonstrated that there was nothing the matter with them save a superabundance of error in their souls. I have learned, too, that she has experienced some dismal failures, notably in the case of the woman with consumption, referred to by Josephine, who, as Winona explained to us, would have got well had she only been able to realize that she was getting better. There was also a patient suffering from mental derangement who grew crazier and crazier, until she was finally carried off by her friends, whereas, as Winona sweetly explained to us, if they had only allowed her to remain a little longer she would have been completely cured, because in Christian Science, as in nature, darkness is apt to be most signal just before the dawn. This diagnosis of the case struck me as highly reasonable. Indeed, I have constantly said to myself that, provided the dear child managed to escape indictment, I had every reason to be contented that she was living up to her lights to the top of her bent. So altogether you can see that my home was a happy one, and that I desired no change.

My two sons-in-law! I see them in my mind's eye walking on either side of me, the one short and slim with a spiritual countenance ; the other tall, handsome, and impressive-looking. Their main object in life seems to be to help me on with my overcoat, and to guide my senile steps over street-crossings, though Dr. Meredith tells me that I am good for twenty years yet, and that I haven't an unsound organ in my body. They disagree with me in politics so politely that I am fool enough to open my best wine when they come to dinner. They dog my footsteps; they silently pass judgment upon me, and I shall never be able to shake them off until I am dead. Why did they come to worry us? We were so happy before we knew of their existence. Out upon them both!

Alas, poor philosopher! Shall I begrudge to my darlings the happiness that I have known in the too swiftly fleeting years of our married life? Love has come to claim my flesh and blood even as it claimed me and Josephine a quarter of a century ago never to loose us from his silken chains. Love the immortal, the transfigurer of souls, the unsealer of eyes which in vain have sought the light which streams from eternity, thou hast come to work anew the old, old story, even though thy coming rends my heart-strings. Down, selfish, stubborn fumes of senile cynicism! I bow to the law of life. Come to my embrace, O sons-in-law; I love you, I bid you welcome to my hearth, even though you regard me as one for whom the grave is yawning! Listen how bravely I call Jim— Jim—Jim, a thousand times Jim. And you, the other one, whose name I do not know, but whose fell purpose I have detected, when your name is divulged to me I will call that too.

X

SAID Josephine to me some three months ago: "Fred, we shall have been married twenty-five years on the twenty-first of next November. We ought to celebrate it in some way."

"How better than by having a silver wedding?"

"Because so many people would feel obliged to give us silver," she replied. "I am perfectly willing, Fred, that people should send me flowers when I'm dead, but I will not have them send silver to my silver wedding."

"The simplest way then would be to tell them not to. Put in the corner of the invitation the letters A. S. W. B. S. B. 'All silver will be sent back.'"

"This is a serious subject, Fred. I should

like very much to have our best friends with us on the anniversary, if I could feel sure that they wouldn't regard it as a tax. We all give willingly when people are married, but it does seem rather a grind, as the children used to say, to have to go out and buy something else a quarter of a century later, when you know that the senile old couple will be able to use whatever you get only a few years at the farthest, and that then it will be snapped up or melted up by their children or grandchildren. Mind you, dear, I should often be glad to give silver myself, if I could afford it ; but I am looking at the matter from the point of view of the world at large. Do you know," she added, "that isn't at all a bad idea of yours. We could put on the cards ' No silver,' just as they put ' No flowers.' It was quite a brilliant suggestion, Fred."

"There are always fools, though, who will disregard such a notice just from sheer contrariness."

"Oh, if we once gave them warning, and they chose to send notwithstanding, it would be their own fault," exclaimed Josephine, buoyantly. "I should hope there would be a few such people, for I should be very glad to have more silver. It's not that I object to the silver, but because I wish to give a loophole of escape to the people who wouldn't send it unless they felt obliged to. I should expect surely to receive quite a lot in one way or another. And it *would* be convenient, love, for Winona did not get any too much when she was married. Everything ran to furniture and books, and out of the little silver she received their were seven large salad forks, all of which had her initials on them, so that she couldn't change them."

There are people who refrain from having their wills drawn on the score that they would be likely to die if they did. While I have no sympathy with this superstition, I must confess that a formal celebration of the twenty-fifth anniversary of your wedding-day has always seemed to me to savor of willingness to have your account with life audited, with a view to being able to sink quietly and becomingly into your grave whenever you were called. In view of the fact that, though each of us has trifling ailments, neither of us is seriously disabled, it seemed a little soon to be taking account of stock and talking of putting up the shutters forever. Yet time's figures are not to be gainsaid, and especially in the Land of Liberty people are not allowed to forget that they are growing old even if they have no tall sons and daughters to attest the fact. What boots it to protest that we feel as young as we ever did? We might be allowed to say so unchallenged, provided we did not try to act on the assumption, but the youths without parents and the newly created species would soon bring us to our senses if we were to assert ourselves in society so as to cause them the slightest inconvenience. The middle-aged are allowed to drive and go to the theatre, and are tolerated at weddings on the ground that they may have given a wedding present, and at garden parties where there is no lack of space, but their room is considered better than their company everywhere else, in spite of the pretty speeches one sometimes hears as to the charm of entertainments where all ages are gathered together, and the glory of growing old gracefully as they do in England. I am not complaining, for between you and me we wouldn't be hired to go to one-tenth of the places to which we ought to be invited, so far as our physical state is concerned ; but it would be soothing to be asked occasionally and not to be treated as though we were moribund, and bidden only to Class Day spreads and to church weddings without a card for the reception. Once in a while lately Josephine and I have taken it into our heads to put in an appearance at the Assemblies, where, though we had been respectfully and cordially received, it has been evident to us that we were regarded as social Rip Van Winkles, and that at least half the company were inquiring who in thunder we were, and the remainder, who did know us, were wondering why in time we came.

A remark of Josephine's served to crystallize these reflections. " Do you know, Fred, that I think on the whole we shall have a happier day if we pass it quietly together, and simply have the children to dine. So many of the people of whom we were fond at the time we were married have passed away, that I am sure we should be appalled by the thinness of the ranks when we began to reckon who are left. Besides, I don't think that a notice not to bring silver would really protect the poor wretches who didn't wish to bring any. It would seem too evidently to mean that they needn't bring any unless they chose to, but that it would be acceptable all the same, which would worry dreadfully those who like to do whatever others do. Don't you think so? You see everybody understands that nobody really objects to receiving silver. Besides, it would involve no end of fuss, and we should be so occupied with the arrangements that we should forget to pay any attention to each other, so that it would be a dreary day to look back upon."

"Indeed, Josephine, I agree with you entirely," said I. "Unless such affairs go off just right they are stiff and ghastly. People who are bent on paying us a compliment will have an opportunity to come to our funerals before very long."

"Not together, though. Oh, Fred, wouldn't

it be the crowning thing of all, after so much happiness, if we *could* die at the same time and never know what it was to miss each other!"

Although we are jointly and severally aware that the years have been slipping away, and that our turns to bid farewell to this dear earth may come any day now despite the fact that we feel young as ever, we choose still to regard death as a shy visitor which is likely to prefer others to us. I say to myself that people rarely die of rheumatism, which is Josephine's only cross, and though pneumonia is a fell destroyer, I know that Josephine is firmly convinced that the colds to which I am subject never attack my lungs. Some day one of us will wake up and miss the other, unless my darling's prayer that we be taken away together be granted; but until we do, are we not happier for cherishing the delusion that we are to be overlooked indefinitely?

Was it a delusion, too, which made my darling, as I helped her into our top-buggy on the morning of our twenty-fifth anniversary, seem to me no less beautiful than on the day when we plighted our troth at the altar? Did she not wear the same sweet, trusting smile, the same noble look in her dear eyes? I told her so, and she informed me that I was demented, but I know she knew that I thought she had not changed, which I am sure was enough for her even if Providence has dimmed my eyes. Yet I maintain that I am right. She is a little stouter, of course; I can see a wrinkle and a crow's foot here and there; and her hair is grizzled. But to all intents and purposes she does not look a day older.

It was a glorious morning; one of those mild, mellow days of the late autumn, when unscientific people wag their heads and proclaim that the climate is changing. There was scarcely a breath of wind, and the landscape toward which our steady nag trotted sturdily wore a faint atmosphere of saffron haze, as though the sunlight had been steeped in the lees of the yellow foliage. And the day we were married there was a driving snowstorm! Josephine had predicted so confidently that history would repeat itself on our anniversary, that I think she was rather disappointed when she awoke to find the sun shining and all the elements at rest.

Our Pegasus scarcely needed the guidance of the reins. He knew where we were going, and sped along with our comfortable if old-fashioned top-buggy at a stylish yet self-respecting gait in keeping with the dignity of the occasion. Our first destination was the attractive home of our daughter Winona, who lives eight miles out of town, on a hundred lordly acres. She has an adoring husband—the tall, handsome, impressive-looking youth of my prophetic soul—and an adored infant six months old. Her husband is a scion of one of the oldest and wealthiest families in the city, and he has already made his mark in the political field. He has been a Congressman, and his admirers are talking of giving him the next party nomination—not my party (so you see that my partiality does not proceed from political affiliation)—for Governor. He is altogether a delightful young man; and as for the baby—.

Josephine broke in upon my rhapsodies over my grandson to say again, for about the fiftieth time during the last year:

"To think, Fred, that though you saw him face to face, you never realized that your magnificent unknown was merely Harold Bruce, whom you had seen and shaken hands with under our roof time and time again. I laugh whenever I think of it. You gave me a fright that day, when you told me that you had run across Winona in the company of a mysterious stranger, which I haven't fully recovered from yet, in spite of the fact that everything has turned out so well. I dreamed that night that she had married a professional gambler, who cut her throat in the course of the first six months because the dear child refused to aid and abet his nefarious schemes."

I replied, meekly, for the fiftieth time, something as to the agonies I had undergone for several years in trying to distinguish one young man from another when they had presented themselves at my house in stereotyped evening dress and done me the honor of squeezing my hand so hard that it was evidently in mistake for the hand of one of my girls. But though my plea has a sardonic look, the words were spoken on this day of days—even as Josephine's were spoken—with an air of gentle, joyous reminiscence, as though, which was indeed the case, we found delight in reviewing again and again the details of the great happiness which has been granted to us in the marriage of our beautiful daughter to one worthy of her.

We drove up the long avenue of tall, stately pines, and found her sitting with her husband and their little hostage to fortune enjoying the glorious mellow sunshine. The tiny monarch sat in his wagon playing with a handful of autumn leaves which his father, with proud paternal indifference to the immaculate surface of the silken carriage blanket, had bestowed upon him. I now became the rival—the successful rival—of the rustling autumn leaves. At my instigation his mother freed him from his equipage and a little anxiously yet resolutely laid him in my arms. I dandled him, I chirruped to him, I hummed to him, I encouraged him to gnaw my watch and to claw my mustache, and presently I began to toss him up in my hands and let him down again.

"Be careful, Fred," said Josephine, warningly ; and I saw a shadow of solicitude cross my daughter's face, though she was plainly doing her best to seem unconcerned.

"Pooh," I answered. "I tossed up all my own babies in this way year in and year out, and not one of them ever got a scratch. I'm not going to begin by letting my precious grandson fall. Am I, little lamb?"

Thereupon, by way of showing what an adept I was in the art of baby tossing, I shot him upward with self-confident impetus. To be sure, my hands never really left him ; they followed him as he ascended and as he came down. Still, pride, the traditional precursor of falls, stood me in bad stead, as it has stood others before me. Just as my precious grandson was descending for the third time, one of my wrists seemed to turn or give way, destroying thereby the admirable balance maintained by my hands, and, quick as thought, Master Baby slipped from my grasp and tumbled to the ground.

A horrible wail of mingled pain and fright, which wrung my heart-strings, welled from the lips of the little lamb, as mother, father, and grandmother rushed to raise him, knocking their own heads together in the process. Harold, white as a sheet and with a son-in-law's curse, as I imagined, trembling on his lips, succeeded in picking him up. I could discern that my grandson's bald little head was dabbled with blood. His mother evidently perceived the same, for she cried, with the maternal fierceness akin to that which we are taught to associate with a tigress protecting its young :

"Harold, give baby to me, and run for the doctor."

Why is it that at the most solemn and serious junctures of life thoughts wholly irrelevant to the occasion will arise without our bidding and thrust themselves into disconcerting prominence ? I was not positive that I had not maimed my grandson for life, though I agree that his stentorian yell had relieved my solicitude a trifle. Certainly, it was a moment of cruel torture, which should have precluded every other consideration from my brain than concern for the hapless infant and harsh self-reproach. And yet, as Winona finished speaking, I made the imp of a reflection that she was sending for a doctor in spite of Christian Science, and that the scales of hallucination had fallen from her eyes at the wail of her own flesh and blood. I was even tempted for an instant to hazard the suggestion that, as there is no such thing as matter, there could be nothing the matter with baby, but I bit my tongue in the throes of my disgust at my involuntary levity.

Harold had sped down the avenue like an arrow, but scarcely had he disappeared before the gory streak which dabbled my poor little victim's brow, and which had seemed to my heated imagination almost an arterial outburst, yielded to the whisk of a pocket-handkerchief. Although he still yelled as if his heart would break, I was beginning to reflect that, barring the very slight scratch on his forehead, he was more frightened than hurt, when Josephine suggested, like a true grandmother, the possibility of internal injuries.

My heart began to throb violently once more, and my mouth to taste dry, but Winona came to my rescue.

"Mother," she exclaimed, in a tone of stern impressiveness, "it is of the utmost importance for baby's sake that you shouldn't think anything of the kind, for by thinking that he has any internal injuries you might, or I might, or father might cause the darling to think the same. We ought all to think that he has nothing the matter with him, and then he will soon cease to cry. Come, let us all think of other things and take our minds off baby. Don't even look at him."

We hastened to do as we were bid. I began to whistle cheerily, and turning my back on my precious grandson, called Josephine's attention to the beauties of the landscape in a series of philosophic utterances. As for Winona herself, she was Spartan enough to restore the little lad to his baby-carriage, and to busy herself in reflecting whether the spot of blood on her robin's-egg blue morning wrapper would wash out. Within three minutes more Master Baby had ceased to sob, and was playing contentedly again with the rustling autumn leaves, when the regular practitioner who, it seemed, lived close by, arrived with Harold at full trot. Winona rose to receive him with a sweet smile, and said, with her old serenity : "Baby is quite well, Doctor. We all applied Christian Science principles to his condition, and he finds that he was in error to suppose that he was really hurt. Thank you so much for coming."

I was really too much overwhelmed by this speech to think of criticising, but Josephine evidently suspected me of something of the kind, for she pinched unmistakably my arm. As for the poor doctor, he was smiling in a sickly sort of fashion when my son-in-law, who I am glad to see is something of a philosopher himself, broke in with—

"Since there are no bones broken, the least thing you can do for us, Doctor, is to stay to luncheon. I have opened a bottle of Clos Vougeot in honor of the twenty-fifth anniversary of the wedding of my wife's father and mother."

"Yes, do stay, Doctor," said Winona.

"And I am very anxious that you should come and vaccinate baby next week."

The doctor stayed and drank our health in a bottle of excellent wine, and not a word was said about science of any kind by anyone. As we drove home I remarked to Josephine that I had made two discoveries: first, that I had lost my grip a little, especially in the matter of babies, and secondly, that Christian Science was evidently a convenient doctrine which could be put on or off like a glove as the occasion demanded. Replying thereto my wife said: "Fred, I consider that you had a marvellous escape with that baby, and that Winona bore it splendidly. As for her silly nonsense, she is evidently in the moulting state, and I prophesy that by the time baby has the measles we shall hear no more of it. Harold seems to understand perfectly how to handle her."

That evening we had our four children and our two sons-in-law to dine with us. It was a state occasion. Josephine was in black velvet, and wore the modest diamond star which I presented to her just before we sat down to table. The girls looked superbly in their best plumage, and it seemed to me, as I glanced to right and left from my patriarchal position, that I had every reason to be proud of the four young men who will control the destinies of the family when I am under the sod. Proud not only of my two dear sons, but of my two dear sons-in-law, who, though one is slight and short, and the other impressive-looking and tall, and though both hold absurd political notions with which I have not the slightest sympathy, have so completely won my heart by their devotion to their wives and generally exemplary behavior, that I cannot choose between them. I was in a jovial mood that evening, I can tell you, and there was nothing excellent and rare in my limited but not wholly featureless cellar which my four brave boys did not have an opportunity to sample in honor of Josephine's and my twenty-fifth anniversary.

Just after the cigars were finished there was a ring at the front door-bell, and Sam Bangs came into the dining-room, rather to my astonishment, for I knew that he had not been invited. "How d'y do, Cousin Josephine; how d'y do, Cousin Fred. Many happy returns of the day."

I observed that Sam spoke with a sort of mysterious blitheness, as though he was under the influence of a joke, and I noticed that he whispered something to my daughter Josie in answer to an inquiring glance from her. Just then there was another ring at the door-bell, and presently through the half-open dining-room doors I caught sight of a host of people gayly trooping into the front hall.

"The Philistines are upon thee, Samson," exclaimed Sam Bangs, as I started to rise in my astonisment. "Cousin Fred and Cousin Josephine, a select party of your friends have taken the liberty of celebrating your silver wedding, and are on the way to the drawing-room, where you are requested to join them."

I was too dazed to speak; indeed, I was conscious of a lump in my throat quite inconsistent with a philosophic temperament. Glancing at my darling, I perceived that she was agitated, and straightway the nightmare, which was at odds with her joy, as to how she was to provide a suitable supper for these delightful visitors, took possession also of my brain.

"Sam," she gasped, "how many are there?"

"All the world and his mother, including the youths without parents," answered her provoking relative with a beaming smile.

But Josie, who it seems was in the secret with Sam, and had managed with him the whole affair, put her arms around her mother's neck and whispered, "Don't believe him. Only people who really care for you are coming. The supper is all provided for, mamma. I entered into a conspiracy with your cook, and you needn't give a thought to anything."

We didn't; and we gave ourselves up to the occasion with a right good will. As our daughter had said, only dear friends whose congratulations were precious to us had been invited, and they, to the number of about fifty, filled out our drawing-room wellnigh to overflowing. Most of them had brought silver—shall I say alas! or happily? Generally some pretty trifle which vouched for the sentiment and taste of the gift horse without seeming to tax the poor animal's resources. For instance, Mrs. Guy Sloane brought a silver butterfly intended for a pen-wiper, and my old friend Sam Bolles a silver paper-knife. Polly Flinders (I never remember her married name), who has babies of her own, gave Josephine a silver whistle, ostensibly intended for my grandson, and Gillespie Gore handed me, with his best bow, an antique silver decanter label marked "Madeira." To be sure, Mrs. Willoughby Walton did bring a splendid Indian silver necklace of exquisite workmanship, which she hung about Josephine's neck with a grand air, informing her that it had once belonged to a princess. As Josephine said to me later, Mrs. Willoughby can afford to be munificent if she chooses, and the necklace will just suit Winona's style of beauty.

Supper was served at half-past ten, and no one would have guessed that my darling had not ordered it. Our healths were drunk, and the healths of our children and grandchild, and I was badgered finally into rising and making a few scattering remarks by way of grateful acknowledgment. An effort of this kind would be trying to the sensibilities of even a real philosopher, and I will confess that, what with stammering and repeating myself, I was uncertain for some moments whether I should be able to make myself intelligible. At last, however, a sudden reflection coming straight from my heart drew me from the slough of renewing thanks and unsealed my lips.

"If," I said, "kind friends, you behold me in my fifty-fifth year a contented man, tolerably well preserved, and with the lustre of true happiness shining from my eyes; if you see around me brave sons and fair daughters, with whose promise of usefulness as men and women you are not ill-pleased; if, indeed, there is any good or any virtue in me or mine, know as the source, the fountain-head, the inspiration of it all, the sweetest woman in the whole wide world, there she stands, my wife Josephine."

As I sat down amid a tumult of approbation, my darling's confused but happy smile shone like a beam from heaven athwart my misty gaze. I see it still as I sit here tonight, with her hand in mine in our silent but joyous home. The mystery of mysteries, life ! Why were we born ? We do not know. What is to become of us when we go hence ? We have no knowledge, but we live in hope. I live in hope. When the last trump sounds, and the graves give up their dead ; when the myriads of souls are brought face to face with God to learn the solution of all mysteries, I shall seek only for Josephine. That I may behold her then is all that I ask of eternity. If I do not see her sweet face, it will be not because I am perfect, but because I have sinned too much.

www.ingramcontent.com/pod-product-compliance
Lightning Source LLC
Chambersburg PA
CBHW021837230426
43669CB00008B/1001